MW01490561

In the Shadow of the Matterhorn

Dave —
Enjoy the memories!! dg
Best wishes —

2013

In the Shadow of the Matterhorn

Intimate Stories about Life, Love, and Laughter at Disneyland

By David W. Smith

In the Shadow of the Matterhorn:

Intimate Stories of Life, Love, and Laughter at Disneyland

By David W. Smith

Published by
SYNERGY BOOKS PUBLISHING
WWW.SYNERGY-BOOKS.COM
P.O. BOX 911232
St. George, UT 84791

All rights reserved. No part of this book may be reproduced or transmitted in any form or by any means, electronic or mechanical, including photocopying, recording, or by any information storage and retrieval system without written permission from the author, except for the inclusion of brief quotations in a review.

Cover art by David W. Smith

Copyright © 2012 by David W. Smith

ISBN: (13) 978-0-9832616-4-3 (10) 0983261644
(Paperback Edition)
Digital/Electronic: (13) 978-0-9832616-5-0

Dedication

This Book is dedicated to my Cast Member Friends; Meaningful friendships that have stood the test of time! It is also dedicated to my Disneyland Canoe Team: *Bad News Canoes* as well as my father, the late Bruce Smith.

Appreciation

Special thanks go to my editor, Caroll Shreeve. Also, to my friend, Ridge Beamis—aka "Beautiful".

Disclaimer

Walt Disney Company Trademarks: **In the Shadow of the Matterhorn** is in no way authorized by, endorsed by, or affiliated with the Walt Disney Company, Inc., Disneyland Park, or WED. Disneyland Park is a registered trademark of the Walt Disney Company. Other trademarks include but are not limited to: Disneyland, Matterhorn Attraction, Tom Sawyer Island, Swiss Family Tree House, Tarzan Tree House, WED, Davey Crockett Explorer Canoes, Magic Kingdom, Critter Country, Pirates of the Caribbean, Haunted Mansion, DEC, Jungle Cruise, Indiana Jones, New Orleans Square, Great Moments with Mr. Lincoln, It's a Small World, Primeval World, Carousel of Progress, Rainbow Ridge Mine Train, Big Thunder Mountain, French Market, Club 33, Blue Bayou, Mark Twain, Columbia Sailing Ship, Mine Train Thru Nature's Wonderland, Cascade Peak, Main Street USA, Mary Poppins, Mickey Mouse, Minnie Mouse, Pluto, Sleeping Beauty's Castle, Coke Corner, Aladdin, A Whole New World (song), Space Mountain, Tomorrowland, Matterhorn Bob Sleds, Fantasyland, Frontierland, Adventureland, Astrojets, Buzz Lightyear, Star Tours, Hungry Bear Restaurant, Disneyland Railroad, Fritter, Splash Mountain, Enchanted Tiki room, Disneyland Hotel, Submarine Voyage, Bear Country, Mickey Mouse, Walt Disney. All references to such trademarked properties are used in accordance with the Fair Use Doctrine and are not meant to imply this book is a Disney product for advertising or other commercial purposes.

The Author assumes no responsibility or liability for damages resulting, or alleged to result, directly or indirectly from the use of the information contained herein.

All images used were chosen from Public Domain Sources or from the Author's Personal Photographs, (except those identified by source permissions).

Foreword

By Lynn Barron
Creator of "The Sweep Spot"

Growing up 20 miles from Disneyland in Lakewood, California, like author David Smith, I often went to Disneyland as a kid. Every time my father would drive our family to Disneyland, I would feel my excitement grow as soon as Matterhorn Mountain became visible through the car window. It was always the same: The vision of that mountain meant more to me than just rides and shows. It meant *MAGIC!*

Later in life, I purchased an Annual Pass and visited the Magic Kingdom more often. I began taking in even more of what the Park had to offer, experiencing Disneyland with older, more mature eyes, and yet, still seeing the "magic" the Park offered every time I went.

Finally, I was hired to work within the "shadow of the Matterhorn" for a total of eleven years: from 1991 to 1993 and 1998 to 2007. The "Happiest Place on Earth" became my employer. It was, in some ways, the happiest 'dream come true' job.

From my earliest recollection, I always held admiration for Disneyland and wanted to know everything I could about it: What was behind that door? Was there something behind that wall? Or, how does that work? Obviously, after working at the Park, I eventually found out many of the answers to my questions. Yet, learning such things didn't ruin the magic for me. On the contrary, it only made me respect and admire the imagination and hard work that went into every aspect of Disneyland on a new level.

Being a cast member at Disneyland was very special and even something to brag about. When telling someone where I worked, I would almost always get an impressed look or smile. Cast members are just one of the many factors separating Disneyland from other theme parks; Disney has long been known for its incredible guest services. Indeed, we were "cast members" not employees.

Every day, working at Disneyland offered a sense of adventure. No matter where you worked in the Park, over the years you would experience surprising occurrences; unique events that created the opportunity for interesting stories to share. As most current and former cast members who read this book will attest, David reveals amazing stories, personal experiences, and anecdotes that capture the spirit of what Disneyland is to so many visitors. Non-Disneyland cast members will truly enjoy an "insiders" view of the Park through David's poignant and personal narration within these pages.

Like David, I too worked with some amazing people at Disneyland and formed friendships that continue today. Reading this book brings back memories of both visiting the Park as well as my eleven years being one of those cast members. While many of the events that we would experience at Disneyland were memorable, it was the friendships that we developed over our time working at the Park that indeed stood the test of time.

It was almost divine intervention that I am writing this foreword for David's book. Living in St. George, Utah, my wife visited the annual Dickens Festival held there, an extensive craft and Christmas show themed around the Dickens story. Excitedly, she came back and presented me with a book called **Hidden Mickey** that she purchased from the author's booth at the festival. The book was the first of a series of action/adventure novels about Walt Disney and Disneyland written by David W. Smith and his co-author, Nancy Temple Rodrigue. The book was a first of its kind mystery about Disney leaving behind a secret diary that is discovered forty years after his passing—a book that contained a cryptic clue to a hidden treasure. I was intrigued by the book as it was not only written for more advanced readers, but it also delved into authentic areas of Walt Disney's history. Even more interesting to me, the book presented elements of Disneyland, both onstage and backstage of which I was familiar with.

As fate would have it, I then ran across David at the D23 Expo in Anaheim in 2011, (a convention for Disney fans from all around the world). I asked him if he would be a guest on a podcast that I host called The Sweep Spot. On the show, my co-host, Laura, and I talk about Disneyland history, touring, tips, and our personal stories working at Disneyland. Having David on the show was a treat for our listeners. He discussed engaging stories about Disneyland and the "story within the story" of how he came up with the idea for his book, *Hidden Mickey*. (*Hidden Mickey* now is a five-volume set!) As with many of our guests on the show, we learned some things from David that we had never known before. *In the Shadow of the Matterhorn* reminds me of our show with David. His book brings to light so many fascinating events and stories that you can't help but want to read more.

When David asked me if I would write a foreword for his new book, essentially a non-fiction memoir of experiences, unpublished stories of working at Disneyland, and intriguing incidents there, I immediately accepted.

Upon reading the draft of *In the Shadow of the Matterhorn*, the book brought back many familiar memories of my experiences as both a guest and as a cast member. It was a trip down several memory lanes. I can't help but think that his words will inspire similar remembrances for all readers, captivating all who have set foot in Walt Disney's Magic Kingdom.

I know that no matter what your own history is with Disneyland, you too will thoroughly enjoy this unique book. Get ready to be given a 'VIP Tour' of Disneyland, one that will touch your 'inner child' and simultaneously tickle your funny bone. Certainly this book is a tour that isn't in any guide book or trip planner. *In the Shadow of the Matterhorn* is a personal tribute to the many lives touched by Walt Disney and his Magic Kingdom of Disneyland.

Enjoy the adventure!

Lynn Barron – 2012
The Sweep Spot
www.TheSweepSpot.com

In the Shadow of the Matterhorn

Introduction
By David W. Smith

While Walt Disney's *Disneyland* held awe and mystique for people who lived well outside of the Shadow of the Matterhorn, those of us who grew up in the vicinity of Disneyland generally took for granted the national and even international appeal and charm that the Park offered regional outsiders. While we all understood and appreciated the allure Disney's *Magic Kingdom* offered all who visited, locals often saw Disneyland more as an upscale city park but with much better slides and teeter-totters. (And an admission price.)

When we did visit the Park, we seldom took a lot of pictures, or even had cameras with us, which further demonstrated our taking Disneyland for granted, consciously or otherwise. However, many of us could recite the entire audio narration to Adventure Thru Inner Space, word for word, ("Will we go on shrinking forever, ever, ever, ever…?") and the Haunted Mansion's spiel, ("Is this room actually stretching? Or is it your imagination?). Some of us knew the Park like the back of our own hand. Adventure for us might include seeing how many people you could drop pennies on from the Skyway or who could stay hidden the longest while playing Hide-and-Seek on Tom Sawyer Island.

We seldom did "touristy" things. We bypassed all the shops, didn't admire the beautiful swans in the moat surrounding Sleeping Beauty's Castle, and we never went on "It's a Small World," (unless it was really hot outside.).

However, now as a fifty-something adult, I look back on my youth of growing up in the Shadow of the Matterhorn with not just nostalgic retrospect, but I now see how the 'House the Mouse Built' was literally influential in defining my life and having a lasting effect on me in so many ways. I could not have guessed that Disneyland would enter so many stages of my life. Likewise, I'm sure the lives of countless other people were also intimately intertwined with Disneyland.

From my earliest recollections of my grandmother taking my sister and me to Disneyland, I have snippets of memories that are as fresh as if I experienced them yesterday. With both my parents working, it fell onto the shoulders of Grandma Marie to spoil her only grandkids by taking them to Disneyland a number of times each year. While I can still picture so many things about those early trips to the Park, there are some memories that have receded far into my consciousness that they are more like fading dreams that I sometimes wonder if any of them are even real.

I do remember the feelings I had as a kid, of being like my movie heroes: James Garner in the movie *Up Periscope* or Kirk Douglas in *20,000 Leagues under the Sea*, when I had gazed out through the oval portals while on the Submarine Voyage at Disneyland. Viewing the vastness of that "liquid space," (or, at least nine million gallons of heavily chlorinated water), as a kid while on the Submarine ride, the voyage was as real to me as if I were exploring the Mariana Trench in the Pacific Ocean alongside oceanographer Jacques Cousteau.

And how could any kid not feel the same sense of adventure that Tom and Huck must have felt—as depicted by the writings of Mark Twain in his book *The Adventures of Tom Sawyer*—while at Disneyland exploring the caves on Tom Sawyer Island, or climbing up in Tom and Huck's Tree-house, or watching the majestic triple-decker Mark Twain Steamship paddle wheeling by with its resonating steam whistle filling the Park with its iconic call?

I have memories of my sister and I sitting very statuesquely so a cast member in one of the Main Street shops could cut our profile out of a piece of white construction paper, and then marveling at not just the likeness of us, but the fact the artist was able to capture the cowlick of hair that protruded like vintage television antennae at the back of my head in the caricature.

In reality, I look back at my experiences with Disneyland in significant stages: Growing up as a kid with my sister and grandma, visiting the Park as a young guest; my teen years of wanting to ride the Matterhorn over and over and later Space Mountain, that was, until we discovered girls! Then came my college years and beyond, working at Disneyland—six years in all—making life-long friendships and learning probably as much about the opposite sex as I learned about Walt Disney during those years.

I recall how each summer would be kicked-off with a dozen Grad Nites, and working shifts from 10:30 pm to 4:30 am. With eyelids that felt like sandpaper against my corneas, I somehow survived the sea of teens that descended on the Park like wide-eyed, formally dressed young adults, yet slowly transformed into walking zombies by closing time. Cast members sometimes resembled zombie-like creatures by 4:30 in the morning, too.

During those six years working at Disneyland I operated rides like Pirates of the Caribbean, the Davy Crocket Explorer Canoes and the Mike Fink Keel Boats. One year, my last summer in fact, I drove the Monorail. Each 'attraction,' (at Disneyland, there were no 'rides' only **attractions**), offered not only different experiences for the guests who partook in each, but each of those attractions also offered the cast members, (another Disneyfied term for "employee"), equally unique experiences and responsibilities. Where else could you pilot a submarine below the Artic Pole, motorboat along the jungle-rivers of Africa, or make the jump to Light Speed and arrive on the far moon of Endor? For the most part, all of us who worked at Disneyland identified the unique positions we held as something special: From the sweeper to the ride operator, from the food service personnel to those working in merchandise, entertainment, maintenance, and landscaping, each job description offered a more unique working environment than most any other employment opportunity that could be found near or far.

At Disneyland, I learned how to control large numbers of guests in many situations, a skill that would be instrumental in my ability to speak publicly without being nervous and even remain relatively comfortable in front of large groups of people. These skills contributed to my ability—and comfort—in performing magic to large audiences as well as playing bass and guitar in front of thousands of people in various nightclubs and venues.

A number of years later—and yet, another stage in my relationship with Disneyland—I had become a high school teacher in Southern California. I returned to the Park as a chaperone for our school's annual senior Grad Nite, which I survived this time by imbibing in large quantities of black coffee and snacking endlessly on popcorn.

Many years later, my Disneyland experience changed dramatically again; I experienced it through the eyes of my young children. Excited to show them the attractions I used to work on, see the fireworks, or meet Mickey Mouse, I donned the role of tour guide with relish and delight.

I would never have guessed that years later, I would write novels that would involve Walt Disney and his beloved Park, Disneyland; my *HIDDEN MICKEY* mysteries emboldened my memories of all the stages of Disneyland experience I had amassed, coupled with imagination and, hopefully, creating intriguing story lines for readers of all ages as a result.

This book is a personal retrospective 'life-book' of Disneyland memories, one which I hope will inspire memories for readers who have had similar interactions with Disneyland or can relate in some way to the personal portrayals I've recounted here.

There have been many books written about Disneyland, from historical perspectives to stories of cast members and various events that have shaped the history of the Park. Like those books, *In the Shadow of the Matterhorn,* is written with a passionate, introspective love and appreciation of Disneyland, not just from a chronological or historical epitome of simple factual events, trivia, or situations, but from my very personal and intimate association with the Park. The events in this book are all true to this author, and many are probably also true for countless others who may have shared similar experiences. My goal—and enjoyment—in writing this book was to bring to life those events, to share some unique Disneyland trivia, and especially, to share some of the wild situations that I encountered over the years through circumstance, fate, or simple luck!

So climb into your 'Doombuggy', 'Atommobile', or 'Astroblaster', or just step up to the yellow line and watch out for the doors in front of you as they swing out. Please remain seated and remember to keep your hands and arms inside the vehicle at all times.

Oh, and please, no flash photography!

Enjoy the Ride!

David W. Smith
December, 2011

Chapter 1

The Curiosity Years: The 1960s

Riding my bicycle the short distance to my elementary school on a relatively cool November morning back in 1964, I could see my breath with each exhale; a momentary cloud of fog issuing forth from my lips then evaporating as fast as it had appeared. I remember gazing down West Street, to the vanishing point of the road where it extended north toward the distant snow-capped peaks of Mt. Baldy that stood a good fifty miles away. The 10,000-foot summit, easily visible on a clear day, was dwarfed, however, by the close proximity of another snow-covered mountain top: that of Disneyland's Matterhorn Mountain.

Foreground: Disneyland's Matterhorn Mountain. To the north, in the background, Mt. Baldy

Rising up in the center of what was still a relatively rural area of Orange County, the replica of Switzerland's famed mount was a landmark if not an anomaly. Pedaling along the side of the road, it was easy to view Walt Disney's scaled-back version of the Swiss peak from only a mile and a half away. The phenomenon of parallax made the mountain seem so much more prolific as the reference point of the distinct peak seemed to move relative to the much more distant horizon. The effect created the illusion that the Matterhorn appeared to be mobile, kinetic. Perhaps it was this observation, while I peddled my blue Schwinn Stingray bicycle further up West Street, (which later would become "Disneyland Drive"...where West Street would cross Katella in Anaheim, at the southwest corner of Disney's California Adventure), that drew my eyes to the mountain even more. It was as if the faux mountain had some sort of corneal magnet drawing my attention to the conspicuous landmark no matter where I was on the street.

17

My daily destination—at least during the nine-month school year—five days a week was Crosby Elementary School. Located near the northern boundary of my home city of Garden Grove where it blended seamlessly with the city of Anaheim, Crosby Elementary was only about a mile south of the Magic Kingdom. All of us could easily see the Matterhorn from the front of our school. The iconic Disneyland centerpiece, (at least as far as height was concerned), was, for most of us kids, a variance in topography for sure, but it also served as a not-so-subtle invitation for all who identified the landmark. Disneyland was a world of fantasy; the unnatural location of a seemingly granite monolith in the middle of OUR community certainly enhanced this fantasy perception all the more. And, of course, such perception had all of us begging our parents to take us to the "Happiest Place on Earth."

From that standpoint, I'm sure that to many of our parents, the identifiable mountain in the middle of Orange Country was more like an "attractive nuisance." Yet, I'll bet even the most jaded adult held at least a small amount of secret admiration—if not a childlike fondness—for Walt's mountain and, of course, for his "little Park."

Early construction of the Matterhorn.

For some kids, those who didn't know any better, the Matterhorn was just a natural occurring geographical protuberance. The association of the mountain was perhaps a little like seeing pictures we had been shown in school of the volcano necks that make up spires of rock in the relatively flat valley floor of Monument Valley at the boarder of Arizona and Utah. Most of us were too young to have seen—or remembered seeing—the rising steel girders that made up the superstructure of the man-made mountain, a sight that created as much interest—if not mystic—in those who actually witnessed the birth of the Matterhorn. For those who weren't aware, I'm sure the early Matterhorn, as it took shape, was for a while, something quite inexplicable. Initially, the steel girders didn't resemble anything coherent. The mishmash of angled beams didn't seem to make much geometric or architectural sense.

The equivalent of seeing such an engineering anomaly, at least for me personally was the construction of the Anaheim Convention Center a block south of Disneyland that was completed in 1967. The main arena of the Convention Center had a sloping disk-like structure that truly resembled a flying saucer. To a youngster of the 1960s—when space exploration was still more fantasy than reality—observing the structure from the short distance of one mile from our school conjured up fantastic images of some spaceport being built under the guise of a mild-mannered convention center. This fantasy was similar to the emergence of a snow-capped mountain appearing in the middle of orange and avocado groves six years earlier. The extraterrestrial shape of the convention center arena—like the mountainous form of the Matterhorn, taller than anything around—was, if nothing else, totally 'far out!'

Inside Disneyland, Sleeping Beauty's Castle remained the resonant focal point for visitors who clicked pictures off with their Kodak Brownie 127 box cameras—or a few years later, Kodak Instamatic cameras—while strolling down Main Street for the first time in those early years of Disneyland's existence. When the surrounding trees of the Park were still young and immature, Sleeping Beauty's Castle and later the Matterhorn appeared much larger than they do today. They have become scaled perceptually differently over time as the pines, eucalyptus, and pepper trees continue to grow abundantly within the tenderly maintained environment Disney had created for such foliage. However, standing at an exact $1/100^{th}$ scale of the actual Swiss mountain, the Matterhorn's 147-foot summit dwarfed the 70-foot spired pinnacle of Sleeping Beauty's Castle in size if not peculiarity and wonder.

If it wasn't the size of the mountain that drew one's attention, the excited screams of passengers on the rollercoaster inside the mountain sure would. Little known facts about the Matterhorn Bobsled ride included that it was indeed the first tubular rollercoaster in the world. It was a ride that Walt Disney first envisioned in 1956 after filming *Third Man on the Mountain* in Switzerland and seeing firsthand the actual recognizable mountain. And yes, up until 2001, there really was a basketball court high up inside the mountain, a court used for recreation by the daily Matterhorn mountain climbers between climbs.

All of this trivia about the Matterhorn meant nothing to us kids, back then. We only experienced the thrill of riding the bobsleds that sped along in and out of the mountain. That's what captured our interest at the time, not to mention all that Disneyland itself had to offer!

Growing up in Orange County, California, where seasons were hardly discernible, a ride on a sled or a toboggan down a snow-packed trail was only attainable by driving an hour and a half north to the back side of Mt. San Antonio—better known as Mt. Baldy—to the town of Ridgeline. Finding a road not having been snow-plowed and with the right slope was always a challenge. Yet here in sunny Orange County, one could ride a thrilling simulation of a perfect toboggan run, without having to put on gloves or a jacket! While seemingly zooming along at speeds faster than the actual 15 to 25 miles per hour, anyone could experience the thrill of riding Matterhorn Bobsleds with just an 'E-Ticket.' ("E-Tickets are something I will talk more about later.)

How could a six-year old not be fascinated with a snow-capped mountain rising out of an otherwise flattened landscape? Knowing the mountain was man-made in no way diminished the awe and almost proud ownership we all had in seeing the crest of its peak towering over all the Magnolia, Acacia, and Jacaranda trees that lined our relatively new—if not modest—neighborhood streets. As we grew older, the fascination with the simulated mountain would of course diminish. However, the long-term relationship many of us would have with the Mountain—and with Disneyland—would become more defined. In fact, for a number of people, Disneyland became a livelihood for many and just as it would be a source of joy and excitement for countless others.

Independence and Carefree Lives

In the late 1960s Garden Grove and Anaheim, as well as other nearby cities such as Orange, Irvine, Santa Ana, Tustin, Brea, and Fullerton, were still sleepy little towns. Most such cities were still dominated by orange and avocado groves, strawberry fields, and open land that was bisected in some areas with walls of twisted eucalyptus trees. These enormous trees served as windbreaks for the orchards or provided natural property lines separating the various family farms and acreage. In some of the orange groves, black 'smudge pots' were spaced within the orchard's divisions where on cold winter mornings these oil-burning pots would be lit to radiate warmth and prevent freezing of the citrus. (This was one of the many reasons that we had more smog on winter mornings, perhaps.)

Crime was not a common word in the vernacular of the town dwellers. As kids, we stayed out until the streetlights came on or until we heard our mothers yell our names, announcing to us—and the whole neighborhood—that dinner was ready. If we weren't riding our bicycles around town, we were playing in the street, usually a pick-up game of '500' or 'Over the Line.' These were baseball games that consisted of us trying to hit line drives without hitting our parent's or neighbor's cars parked along the sides of the street. The simple fear of denting a car taught us all how to control our swings, which probably carried over to my ability later to hit tennis balls accurately.

Anyone's home that a basketball hoop on their driveway became a local hangout where constant two-on-two or three-on-three games would be played during basketball season. And when we put up a hoop at seven feet high instead of the regulation ten, we could all slam dunk like the pros. (Even if we were a bunch of short, white kids, and none of us possessing a very high vertical jump.) I remember pretending to be my basketball idol, Jerry West, of the Los Angeles Lakers, aka 'Mr. Clutch,' trying to make a half-court shot at the buzzer to win the game. (Actually, for me, it was trying to make a forty-five foot shot from the manhole cover in the center of my street!)

Yet, nothing matched the freedom we felt when we hopped on our bicycles and explored our communities. Bikes were the prerequisite forerunner to getting our driver's licenses. Inserting playing-cards in the spokes of our bikes was akin to having 'boom tubes' that I would put on my pickup truck's exhaust manifold years later.

Unlike today, back then there were very few overweight kids in our circle of friends. We would hardly bat an eye at riding our bikes twenty miles a day. If we had a water bottle and a candy bar, we could peddle our bikes just about anywhere. And, also unlike today, our parents didn't think twice about letting us go riding all over town. "Okay! Have fun!" was the extent of my mom's expressed concern about our heading out to explore new areas on our bikes.

We would ride our bikes around town, along busy streets, down narrow alleyways, and across open fields. We cruised along the railroad tracks in Garden Grove where they traversed town in a northwest, southeast diagonal line, past the giant, towering silver water tank that proudly proclaimed in bold, black letters, "The City of Garden Grove" on its sides. The water tower, (always reminding me somehow of the Tin Man in *The Wizard of Oz*), stood as its own landmark, rising a good hundred and fifty feet above town. Built in 1926, the water tower was erected near the Garden Grove Citrus Association's orange packing house. It was a central location where Valencia oranges picked from the 30,000 acres of area orange groves would be transported for packaging and shipping. The tower gave all of us kids a point of reference while we rode around; none of us ever got lost anywhere in town.

As we got a little older, on weekends we would ride our bikes south on Harbor Boulevard, and end up at the beach, some twelve miles away. Or we would head east on Chapman Avenue to Irvine Park, challenging ourselves to make the steep grade up toward Orange Park Acres and Orange Hill Restaurant without getting off our bikes and walking. Irvine Park had nice hilly trails to ride on, a lake in the middle where we could rent row boats and a little later, paddleboats became the big fad on the lake.

It was in Irvine Park that one day when I was about eleven years old I went down a hill and squeezed the front brakes on my bike a little too hard. The steep angle of decent and my locking up the brakes on my front wheel, I ended up going head-over-handlebars, landing on my head and back. Back then, no one wore helmets and I really could have been seriously hurt. As it was, I had the air knocked out of my lungs. After a few moments of panic when I couldn't catch a full breath, I calmed down and realized I could still breathe. But, suddenly, I went completely blind! To this day, I don't know why I lost my sight. My friend Mark helped me walk my bike and guided me to a pay phone where, in a panic, I called my dad. By the time my dad arrived with his 1962 Ford Ranchero pickup truck, some of my sight had returned. However, for another hour, everything I was seeing was in black and white; I remember how my limited vision made everything look like the old-time black-and-white film negatives. Eventually—and thankfully—my vision returned to normal and we were back riding our bikes without a care in the world the next day.

Biking to the Park

It wasn't long before our bicycles would bring us closer to the Shadow of the Matterhorn.

Among the locations we picked to ride, we found that the Disneyland Hotel was full of interesting things to do for a bunch of imaginative twelve-year-olds. Riding to Disneyland Hotel, (straight up West Street a mile and a half), was a much shorter ride than peddling to the beach or up the hill to Irvine Park. By the time we were in sixth grade, Disneyland Hotel became our most common destination.

Disneyland Miniature Golf Course and Driving Range

Where the enormous Mickey and Friends parking structure is today, (the main parking structure for Disneyland guests), the Disneyland Driving Range and Miniature Golf Course used to be located. A few years prior, there was even a helicopter landing area for the Disneyland Helicopter Service.

A little before we started riding our bikes to the Disneyland Hotel, there used to be the "Disneyland Helicopter Heliport" which was located just west of the Disneyland Driving Range. A little obscure in Disney history is that Disneyland had helicopter service from Los Angeles Airport to the Disneyland Hotel operated by LA Airways.

While the helicopter service certainly saved time, the reality was that the vehicles were noisy, had limited views for passengers, and the cabin space was cramped. And arguably, they may not have been all that safe.

In 1968, two of the worst civilian copter crashes in U.S. history occurred with the helicopter service. The first crash killed 23 persons and occurred on May 22nd. A second crash on August

14th killed 21 people. Disneyland discontinued service later that year.

When I was very young, we could see the Disneyland Helicopter fly over our house and we would run out to watch it pass by. My mom would tell us, "Wave to the Disneyland Helicopter." The loud, 'whoomp, whoomp, whoomp' of the helicopter flying overhead could be heard from all over the city.

Locking our bikes against a chain-link fence near the entrance of the driving range and putt-putt course, we often would scrounge up the seventy-five cents it cost to play the miniature golf course, challenging each other to make putts through a miniature Sleeping Beauty Castle's draw bridge opening or around fountains of Mickey Mouse and other Disney characters.

My early experience with real golf was here. A large box of used clubs sat near the entrance to the hitting mats of the driving range. Drivers, three-woods, and a mishmash of irons were sticking out of drilled holes in the plywood that covered the top of the box. The dinged and scraped-up clubs were to us kids, an attractive nuisance. Playing sword fighting with the clubs was a common— and short-lived game. Range attendants would ask us if we were going to buy a bucket of balls to hit...and if not, the clubs were not to be used as weapons.

On slow days, we would run out to the driving range grass area and snag a few of the balls that had been poorly hit by previous patrons. We'd then challenge each other to see who could hit their ball the furthest. Since I had a dad who was quite good at golf, and who had shown me how to swing the club correctly, I usually won the long-drive contests. But my best friends, Mark and Tim who were usually my riding buddies, would often connect with a drive that beat me out, making the game a challenge nonetheless.

When we became bored with the golf area, we found shops, at the Disneyland Hotel near the monorail station, that were fun to explore. There was a toy store; we would spend time looking over the cool things that we couldn't afford. In front of the shops was the Disneyland Hotel Monorail Station where we could watch the sleek, futuristic vehicles glide into and out of the station. We always dreamed of having enough money to ride the Monorail to the Park. (It remained a dream for quite a while.)

As we got older, we found that girls liked to visit the shops too. At some point, as I will talk about later, we became more interested in the girls we would see—and sometimes meet—than what the shops had to offer.

Once, we found that there were ice machines out on the side of the hotel on each floor where the exterior stairwells and fire-escapes were. Suddenly, throwing ice cubes as far as we could or hitting objects we would call out such as palm tree branches, bushes several stories below, or signs along the walkways, became a new game. We never aimed at the 'moving targets', (people), as we knew that was certainly grounds for getting us in big trouble. Now, I'm not saying that we were the cause, but a few weeks later upon a return visit to the aforementioned ice machines, we found that they had installed metal grills that covered the previously open balconies. This made it impossible to throw an ice cube anywhere...except down our friends' shirts!

December 15th, 1966

I don't think any of us were aware of who Walt Disney really was at the time. I mean, yes, we knew his name and that he was responsible for Mickey Mouse, Disneyland, and movies like *Mary Poppins* and *Swiss Family Robinson*. But to the best of my recollection, none of us had met Mr. Disney. To me and my friends, he was a name, not a person. No more than President Kennedy was to us in 1963 when he was assassinated in Dallas, Texas. I only mention Kennedy because I remember my kindergarten teacher holding a black and white picture of Kennedy the day he was shot with tears in her eyes; I couldn't understand how a picture of a smiling man could make someone cry.

Death was not something that a little kid was exposed to much back then. We didn't have computers or the Internet to witness all the horrors of near and far. We had grainy black and white televisions that not only were nowhere near the size or definition of television screens decades later, but I think we only had three channels back then. Death was far away; somewhere in a country called Vietnam. People starved to death in some place called Bangladesh, or so we were told in school. To us, death was a whispered secret, something held back from us when a friend of the family or a relative died. It was sort of like when our parents would say something about the 'birds and the bees'—it was almost secret or taboo to talk about death. It also seemed at that time, no one we ever knew died.

However, when Walt Disney died on December 15th, 1966, it was not whispered, it was not a secret, and certainly, it was not a holiday...and it was not on the other side of the world. The newspapers, the few television stations, and the radio programs all drove home the fact that the Master Storyteller was indeed, dead.

Chapter 2

Tickets and Deception

Yes, Walt Disney had died.

However, Disneyland was still open right down the street. As they say in Hollywood, or, in this case, Anaheim, "The show must go on."

I was too young to really understand the effect Walt Disney had on the entertainment world in general. Nor could I really predict the effect that Walt Disney would have on the world decades after his death. In fact, it would be another fifteen years before I would learn firsthand about Walt. And it would be another thirty years until I recognized and appreciated the life-long effect that Walt Disney's life would have on my own and the lives of future friends.

I learned that before I was born, my father worked at Disneyland when it first opened in 1955. He actually had Walt Disney come to his attraction, the "Storybook Land Canal Boats."

The Storybook Land Canal Boats originally opened as "The Canal Boats of the World" but closed after a couple months of problems with the boats themselves. At the time, money was so tight with Walt and Disneyland that none of the miniature world landmarks were even built. Instead, the ride was redesigned and added to over the years to include detailed miniature settings from Disney movies instead.

I have a picture of my father spieling on those boats, which later became an all-female attraction.

At the time, I had no idea that I would follow in my father's footsteps. Years later, my father would relegate me with stories about working the attractions or the Main Gate. Perhaps it was this imprint of history my father bestowed upon me so long ago that led to this book?

The summer of 1967 was when my personal interaction with Disneyland the Park began.

"Have you any spare tickets?"

When we were in the fifth grade, my best friend Mark and I discovered a new summer activity. (No, it wasn't chasing girls...not yet, anyway!)

Our new activity began when one day we were hanging around the Disneyland exit. I remember we used to take the Disneyland Hotel Tram to the Park entrance and mill about the area imagining what it would be like if we had enough money to afford admission and the A – E Tickets that were necessary to go on each ride or attraction. It was a warm summer day when Mark and I were looking through the bars that separated us from the magic of Disneyland, when a family leaving the Park spotted us. The dad caught my attention and asked me if we wanted their leftover Disneyland-ride coupons, probably thinking we were waiting to go into the Park with friends or family members. Even though we had not been in the Park that day, and had no money to pay the Main Gate admission, we gladly took in several ticket books the family offered, each with a number of tickets still inside, including several of the famous 'E-Tickets'. It was almost like being handed crisp, new one dollar bills!

For those not old enough to remember the Disneyland Ticket Books or the E-Ticket, a little back-story here:

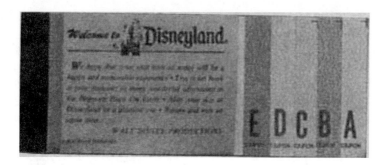

The Disneyland "Coupon" book which included admission and a select number of each A- E coupon; you could purchase books that had different numbers of coupons depending on the number of rides you wanted to go on.

When Disneyland opened in July of 1955, the price of admission was one dollar! However, to go on any of the 'Attractions' you had to have specific tickets. Originally, there were three types, the A, B, and C coupons. A "Day at Disneyland" booklet, which included several of each type of ticket and one Park admission, ran you $2.50. It wasn't until the next year that Disneyland added the "D" ticket as new attractions opened up. But, it was in 1959, the year that Disneyland expanded Tomorrowland, added the Matterhorn, and such classic attractions such as the Submarine Voyage, the Monorail, and the Matterhorn Bobsleds, that Disneyland introduced what would become the famous green "E Ticket."

Perhaps because the E Ticket was green, closer to the color of real paper money or nearly the same color as the game Monopoly's popular $20 dollar bill that the E Ticket was visually so admired. Of course, the real "Value" of the E Ticket came from its association with the rides in Disneyland...the BEST rides required an E Ticket! Its perceived Value created the phrase "That's an E-Ticket..." to describe something of value in the English lexicon. Now, more than thirty years since the E Ticket—and all the specific ride coupons—were abandoned, (in favor of "Unlimited Ride" tickets), we still refer to anything as being very valuable or cool or worth doing as an "E Ticket" item.

The famous "E Ticket"! The rides at the period of time were considered the most popular and best that Disneyland had to offer! Hence, the term "E Ticket" has become synonymous with anything that is considered 'the best!'

Receiving those free tickets that day from the family leaving the Park triggered a collecting or scavenging mentality for my friend Mark and me. Since we never had enough money to get into Disneyland, we considered the acquisition of more and more tickets was almost the same as receiving free money! We figured if those people voluntarily handed over their leftover tickets, well maybe there were a lot more people leaving Disneyland willing to happily hand over their extra tickets too!

We noticed that by late in the afternoon, many people would be leaving Disneyland. Some were leaving to have dinner somewhere outside the Park, while others were leaving for good. Having spent all day there, they were ready to go home. Mark and I, not being shy or introverted in the least, began approaching groups of people leaving and asking them if they were coming back to the Park later. If the answer was no, we asked them if they had any tickets left over that they didn't want. About half of the guests who were not returning offered their extra tickets without a second thought. We learned to avoid asking those guests who went through the exit turnstile that had a sign "Re-entry Stamps". It was through this one turnstile that a cast member would stamp their hand that could be used to re-enter the Park later that day. Such guests obviously were planning on coming back to the Park and even more obviously, would not be willing to give up their leftover ticket books. Most of those exiting the remaining turnstiles were more likely not returning to Disneyland and were far better candidates to ask about any unused tickets.

Eventually, a security guard would come up to us, notice what we were doing, ("panhandling," as we were told), and ask us nicely to leave. We respected authority and of course did as we were told. But, usually not until after we had pocketed dozens of half-spent ticket books!

We always parked our bikes at the Disneyland Hotel and took the free Disneyland Tram to and from the Main Gate. (It was sort of taking a free ride TO Disneyland. Since we couldn't get into the Park, the tram was the closest thing we could do that was like being IN the Park!) While riding the tram back to the hotel, we would tear out the various A through E tickets and count what our haul was for the day. A week or two later, we'd return and repeat the process until we were asked to leave again. It got to the point where the security guards recognized us if they saw us walking up and interceded even before we could ask a single guest for their leftover tickets.

"Not today, boys," I remember one guard in his blue uniform and white security hat saying as we approached the exit gate. We would moan a little, frown, and turn around and head slowly back to the tram. However, we also knew that the security guards would rotate positions around the Park every shift. So, we would simply return twenty or thirty minutes later and we find ourselves able to 'work the guests' for a while until asked to leave again by another guard.

We found out that the guards didn't like to make any kind of scene with any guests, even those of us who were 'guests-wanna-be's! So, while we knew we were doing something we shouldn't be doing, we learned the worst that could happen to us was a simple request for us to leave. Never were we escorted to the security office and had our parents called. Perhaps it was because even though we knew we were doing something wrong, we were always very polite and we respected the security guards. Never once did we cause any disturbance. The moment we were asked to leave, we always did.

The Mother Lode

One day, after successfully obtaining a number of leftover ticketbooks and waiting for the tram to arrive to return us to the hotel to retrieve our bikes, we were sitting on the bench when an older lady came up to us asking, "You boys aren't collecting Disneyland Tickets, are you?" I think what we were doing was pretty obvious since we were tearing out the tickets from each book. We had a bunch of discarded empty coupon books piled next to us on the bench.

We weren't sure if she was part of Disneyland in some way and that perhaps it was against some obscure rule that you couldn't collect tickets from guests leaving beyond the fact they didn't like any panhandlers bugging the guests as they left. However, we honestly—if not sheepishly—replied, "Yes, ma'am, we are."

Anticipating some sort of trouble or a call out to security, we were surprised when she called out to a large group of people standing nearby waiting for the same tram we were waiting on. Imagine our surprise when after a brief discussion by the woman who had approached us and the group of people that had joined us, each person started digging into their purses and pockets for left over ticket books and started handing them to us! It turned out that they were all part of a large family reunion from some far-away place and none were planning on coming back to the Park anytime soon.

I'm sure our excited "Thank You" to each person portrayed our enthusiasm and appreciation. By the time we counted all the tickets collected that day, we had almost fifty tickets. More importantly, there were a number of valuable E Tickets in each of those books that day! Talk about excitement.

After each day, we divided our treasure drove of tickets evenly between the two of us. At one point, I had in my personal collection over one hundred E-Tickets and at least two hundred of the other A thru D tickets in my stash!

Disneyland used to sell a 'Mystery Box' with a picture of the Haunted Mansion on the outside. The box had a secret compartment, which posed the 'mystery' of how to open it. You had to slide different sections of the box around in a specific order to finally open the compartment. This was one of the few things I ever purchased at Disneyland...but it kept my most prized possession: My collection of Disneyland Tickets!

Getting IN!

Having a ton of E-Tickets was really of little significance since they could only be used INSIDE Disneyland. Everyone who knew of our growing pool of tickets admired our collection...but, the question always came up, "When are you ever going to USE those tickets?"

It wasn't long after we started to collect tickets that we were actually able to take advantage of them. They say 'necessity is the mother of invention;' and the need to use the tickets in the only place they were good became the challenge for our next activity!

As I mentioned, we knew from standing near the exit gate all those times asking departing guests for leftover tickets, that people who wanted to come back to the Park later that day not only never gave up their tickets to us, but that they always got their hand stamped at the exit and returned later that day or evening. The hand-stamp ink was a special invisible liquid that not only had an interesting fragrance but also formed a secret, invisible Disney word. When shown under a phosphorescent or "black light" lamp, the hand stamp name would be visible to the attendant checking hand stamps at the re-entry gate, which allowed the guest to return to the Park.

Curiously, we went over to the re-entry turnstile and watched the man or woman working the gate as they checked hand stamps of people returning to the Park. From here, we could see the hand stamps that came through. It suddenly dawned on me after seeing the color of the ink under the phosphorescent lamp that the special liquid Disneyland used for the hand stamp was nearly the same color of a phosphorescent paint I had at home, which I used for painting black-light posters. Remember, this is back in the early 1970s. I think every kid in that generation, around the turn of that decade, had at least one 'black-light poster' in their room. If you didn't have a "Peter Max" poster, you had one of those phosphorescent posters of a sailing ship or a field of space or something!

In my bedroom, I had a large four-foot long black light my dad installed above my closet doors. I'd turn off all the lights in my room at night, turn on that black light, and gaze around my room as all the black-light posters seemed to ignite in glowing colors against their black backgrounds.

A store at the local mall sold a set of black-light paints, water-based phosphorescent colors you could use to paint your own black-light poster. I had a set of those paints at home, which Mark and I began experimenting with the colors on the back of our hands. We noticed the blue paint of the paint set was almost exactly the same color under the black light as the invisible ink used by Disneyland for their hand stamps when shown under their black light.

The problem was, our paint was clearly visible when painted on paper or on the back of our hands. We knew this would not work if we were going to try and 'counterfeit' the Disneyland hand-stamp ink. Our paint would be seen before we could get our hands under the black-light. However, we also knew that many people's stamps became faint because they took showers or went swimming at their hotel swimming pool before returning to the Park. So we tried blotting the painted letters with a wet tissue after writing a word on the back of our hand. We blotted our hands until the paint was hardly visible. Surprisingly, as we found under my black-light at home, there was still enough of the paint in the pores of our skin to still be visible—and readable! In fact, after blotting, our "stamp" looked virtually identical to the hand stamp ink we had seen on the back of the various hands of guests re-entering Disneyland.

Problem one was solved: We had devised a way to create the hand stamp ink image for the re-entry gate of Disneyland.

The second problem was finding out what name was used for the daily hand stamp because it changed every day. We knew the names were characters from Disneyland: Mickey, Minnie, Donald, Pluto, Goofy, and such. We had to find out what name was being used on any given day that we wanted to get into the Park. We couldn't very well just paint on the name standing next to the re-entry gate!

We solved this problem by having one of us stand near the re-entry gate, pretending to be waiting for someone. We would strike up a conversation with the person working the gate, telling them we were waiting to meet our family at that spot. Casually, we would ask what the stamp said that they were checking on the back of each person's hand. Naturally, the worker would show us the hand of someone coming in or we would simply look over out of curiosity and observe a person re-entering the Park. We usually could see right away the name being used for the day. Once we knew the name of the stamp, a quick, "Oh, there they are," we would shout and run off as if we had spotted our family. Problem two solved: We knew what the day's hand-stamp word was!

There was a set of restrooms just behind the waiting area of the Hotel Tram to the west of the Park entrance. Thankfully, the restrooms were seldom used. It was here, in the men's restroom, we began our artwork. I had put a small amount of the blue black-light paint inside one of those black plastic film canisters since I didn't want to lose my jar of black-light paint while at the Park—or worse, getting caught with the paint! We brought a couple of toothpicks with us to serve as impromptu paint brushes. We found that the tip of a toothpick worked better at drawing the letters on the back of our hands than any paint brush.

One of the hard parts to printing the hand-stamp name on our hands was matching the small peculiarities each stamped name hand. We had tried to look closely at the name of the hand stamps being checked at the re-entry gate. What we saw was that each stamp had some embellishments to the word in the form of small lines or curly-cues coming off some of the letters. However, after seeing the stamps many times, we got to the point where we could master the exact look of the stamp for each name. The hardest name to do was "Donald" since it was the most letters. We loved it when the name was "Pluto" or "Snow" or "Goofy." But, for some reason, the extra letter in Donald made it hard to get the printing correct. It wasn't just the extra lines for "Donald". Our trouble came in the width of the word. Often, we would paint the letters too close or too far apart. Washing it off completely, we would have to start over several times until we were sure the name looked as good as the official stamps.

One of the most difficult parts was that we didn't have a handy, portable black-light with us to inspect our stamps before trying to use them at the re-entry gate. However, the practice we had done at home under our own black-light provided us with a certain degree of confidence.

We also began to notice that often many, if not most, of the guest's hand stamps were far less legible than our own! We started making ours even more faint and even left off part of the word sometimes because so many other stamps simply didn't get stamped all the across many of the hands by the person stamping hands at the exit.

After blotting the visible paint from the back of our hands, we were ready to "do the deed" and sneak in!

Waiting in the re-entry line of guests for our turn to show our hands under the black light was akin to waiting to get caught robbing a bank. We knew what we were doing was wrong, but we also knew it was a challenge to see if it worked. We were not there to cause problems, so we rationalized our actions.

By the time it was our turn to slide our hand under the black light at the re-entry gate, our hearts were pounding in our chest. We felt sure the attendant could hear the tell-tale thumping of our fear. We tried to look as nonchalant as we could, trying hard not to be too cool, but also not too touristy. We flipped a coin to see who would go first, since we felt that person ran the biggest risk of getting caught. We also split up by several people in line so it looked like we were with other guests, instead of two young boys doing exactly what we were doing—sneaking into Disneyland!

I believe on our first attempt, I lost the coin flip and was the first to go through. I stood in line, waiting for my turn. I reached the turnstile and began putting my hand up under the light. I watched the gate attendant check my hand; he guided my hand up, moving it up closer to the light. This didn't bother me at first since many of the stamps of guests had become faint from swimming and such. We'd seen this procedure before. However, expecting the worse, (as in the attendant calling over a supervisor—or worse, a security guard), I closed my eyes in anticipation of the worst. I was surprised, no, shocked, to hear, "Have a nice time," as the attendant encouraged me to go on through the turnstile. Mark followed me, a few people back, with an equally easy time through. Suddenly we were IN!

I don't think anything inside Disneyland gave us more of a thrill than when we got through that re-entry gate! However, with a stack of our Disneyland tickets we had brought from our collection, the excitement of knowing we could go on any ride, almost as often as we wanted to, was absolutely COOL!

Over time, we learned a valuable hint to ensure our ability to sneak in: One day, ahead of us in the re-entry line, we noticed the gate attendant looking at another guest's hand stamp very carefully...almost as if the stamp was not at all visible. We heard the man ask the guest, "Have you been in the Park today?" with the guest nodding yes. The next question made both Mark and I get out of line: "Have you bought anything in the park today?" We figured the question was asked as it would be proof that the guest had obviously been in the Park if he or she had indeed purchased something while there.

The guest pulled out one of the trademark Disneyland merchandise bags with something in it, and upon its witness, the guest was ushered into the Park without further probing.

We seldom came to the Park with any money: a wad of ride tickets was all we usually brought. However, I think one of us had a dollar or we found some money on the ground that day, and we headed over to the small souvenir stand just outside the Main Gate next to the exit. There we purchased a postcard and a small Mickey Mouse eraser, each for about a dime, and made sure we got two small Disneyland merchandise bags to hold our "souvenirs".

We got back in the re-entry line holding our "Insurance" in our hand-stamped hands. Never once, did we get hassled about our stamps. But holding the little bag of a single post card or a Mickey Mouse eraser gave us a secure feeling that if there was any question of, "Have you been in the Park today" and "Have you purchased anything in the Park today," we had our 'proof'! That postcard and eraser—and subsequent merchandise bag—were carefully folded up and stored inside our pockets and were with us on every excursion to the Park! Ironically, we never once had to resort to showing the bag or the contents. Probably because we simply were holding the bag in our hand as we held our hands up to the black-light saved any inquiry.

Ditch-em!

Those were carefree summer days, at least once we had made it past the main gate! Walking down Main Street, I can still remember the thrill of getting in the Happiest Place on Earth!

What we did each day was sort of a blur in terms of recollecting any specific event or procedure. One thing I do remember very well is when we would play "Ditch-em" on Tom Sawyer Island before it closed at dusk.

In all honesty, Tom Sawyer Island was practically the most perfect location to play a hide-and-seek game for kids. The Island had caves, trails, a fort, a tree house, and probably most importantly, a snack bar.

When there were three of us, the game was wickedly fun. Two, it was much harder and took longer to locate the other person. With three of us, once one person found and tagged one of the others, they would team up and locate the third player. There were places to hide, places to plan an ambush, and lookouts where we could try and spot one another. The goal was to tag the other person from behind when they didn't see you coming. To win, you had to be the last person tagged.

The caves on the Island were the most fun. Injun Joe's Cave, which had a 'bottomless pit' section, stalagmites and stalactites, and a treasure chest that filled the center of one of the larger cave 'rooms' was the shorter of the two caves. There was a second, longer cave, the 'Escape Route' that extended through a secret door inside the Fort and meandered down to the river. On the southeast end of the Island was Tom and Huck's Treehouse, a much smaller treehouse than the Swiss Family Treehouse across the Rivers of America near the entrance to New Orleans Square from Adventureland. (The Swiss Family Treehouse was reworked in more recent years to become the Tarzan Treehouse. However, for those of us who grew up going to Disneyland, this treehouse would forever be the Swiss Family Treehouse.)

After an hour or so of running around chasing each other on Tom Sawyer Island, we spent whatever nominal amount of money we brought with us—or found while cruising the Park—on ice cold lemonades they sold at the fort and at a small snack bar shack on the other end of the Island. Occasionally, one of us found money on the ground, a quarter here or there, dimes and nickels. When we had enough, we bought a 'Fritter', a round clump of deep-fried bread covered in powdered sugar and utterly delicious.

Those were indeed the days. Sitting at the edge of one of the piers that jutted out from the edge of the Island, we pulled our shoes and socks off and sat on the end of the pier with our feet in the water, sipping our lemonades and watching the river traffic. The Mark Twain, Disneyland's iconic steamboat, the Columbia, (a scaled-back replica of the first American sailing vessel that circled the globe), two Keel Boats, and a number of Davy Crocket Explore Canoes moved along the river. People on board the crafts all waved to us, seemingly having just as much fun watching us with our feet in the water as we had watching them sail by.

This scene of us sitting idyllically on the pier with our feet in the water sipping lemonade was so nostalgic for me that I included it at the end of the first chapter of my Disney book, *HIDDEN MICKEY 5: Chasing New Frontiers*.

I remember one memorable afternoon when sitting on the pier that a canoe glided by us. After waving to the people and ride operators on the canoe, the rear guide swung his paddle over his head and brought the blade down onto the water on the side of the canoe facing us. The paddle made a slapping sound against the water's surface. A perfect stream of water shot forth from the contact point of the paddle and the water, arching towards us on the pier. The jet of water landed right at our feet, as if the guy used a water hose to control the distance and direction of the spray. We all thought this was one of the coolest thing we'd ever seen at the Park.

Little did I know that single event would have a lasting impression on me years later.

After seeing that canoe operator do that with his paddle, I wanted to work at Disneyland!

I remember those couple years we found ourselves inside Disneyland, sipping lemonades or going on rides like the Matterhorn or Peter Pan, those were happy and carefree times. After all we were kids being kids! Playing games and riding rides, we rejoiced at how lucky we were. We didn't want anything to change.

But change did come...

I'm not sure when change officially came, but at one point we suddenly became more interested in girls than in playing games or riding rides!

Chapter 3

Discovering the Opposite Sex—Disneyland Style

A different type of Disneyland Magic came unexpectedly while I was at the Park for our eighth-grade graduation.

It was June of 1971.

Like most of the junior high schools in Orange County, there was an annual celebratory afternoon at Disneyland for those who purchased special school tickets. We rode a bus to the Park, lined up outside the Main Gate, and that's pretty much where the sense of organization ended! Once inside the Park, we scattered like bees in a field of colorful flowers. Most of us had close friends who we hung with. I remember being with Mark and a number of other kids as we speed-walked to the best rides in the Park. (Running, of course, was never allowed in the Park!)

It was that lighthearted time of both year and lifetime. We were young, school just finished for the summer, and hormones for most of us were just beginning to kick in. Also, there was that underlying trepidation of starting high school the next year. Ninth grade had all the reputation of being pretty hard on 'scrubs,' the name given to the freshmen. It was also a time of physical change. Well at least for the girls, all who seemed to mature faster than the guys and it was ever so apparent.

For me, it was an awkward time of physical and emotional transition. I was a skinny, lanky kid, showing minimal athletic prowess and even less motivation in dealing with the opposite sex.

Oh, I was interested, but like most of the boys my age I had no clue of how to interact with them.

It wasn't that I didn't notice girls. No, I was observing, very acutely in fact, the curves that most of the girls suddenly possessed. Every day, it seemed more and more, that those curves were overriding anything else in my mind, especially when a girl possessing those curves was near! Even earlier, when Mark and I would sneak into the Park, we began taking more than a passing interest in girls whom we saw wearing shorts, tank tops, or summer dresses. But that was more like 'watching the parade' not being IN the parade!

However, my first real encounter with girls my age, in some naïve sort of interaction, happened at Disneyland that warm, sunny, June afternoon. It was what would become one of many 'twists of fate' directly involved in memorable Disneyland experiences.

In Line in the Shadow of the Matterhorn

Goofing around, a bunch of us made a beeline for the *Matterhorn Bobsleds*, which, at that time, (early 1970s), was the only 'thrill ride' in the Park. All of us were jockeying around to see who would have to sit behind and who would have to sit in front, basically on a seat that was like sitting on the lap of the other person.

As we approached the turnstile, I noticed the cast member who was taking the necessary "E-tickets" from the guests, was preoccupied with the other line that fed into the Matterhorn attraction. With two tracks, there were two lines that snaked around the base of the mountain and then came together at two turnstiles where a single cast member stood between them, taking tickets. I pushed through the turnstile quietly, without giving my E-Ticket to the young cast member who was turned the other way. It appeared to me that the guy didn't seem to notice me. After pushing through, I tried to act like I had given the guy my ticket, looking away and moving as close to my friends already inside the final queue area that preceded the actual loading dock. Now, you would think that a guy like me, who had probably more E-Tickets than anyone in Orange County, wouldn't care about giving up an E-ticket. Yet, I guess it was the whole idea of getting in free that made me do what I did! Unfortunately for me, the ride operator didn't just fall off the turnip truck! He looked at me and I could feel his eyes on the back of my head. I turned finally and gave him a 'what?' look.

"Ticket?"

"I gave it to you."

"Uh huh," the guy said with a sly look on his face.

Next thing I know, I'm standing outside the ride looking at my friends.

The cast member had kicked me off the ride!

I simply stood there, mouth agape, an incredulous look on my face, I'm sure.

Suddenly, I was left out, watching my friends finish the short queue to the loading area and then laughingly getting in the Bobsleds. I felt foolish and a little devastated and long forgotten by my friends.

What did I expect? All of them come rushing to my defense? Hey, we're talking thirteen-year-old boys, here! Each shrugged before the line moved them well away from me.

Just outside the entrance to the *Matterhorn Bobsleds* was a planter with an iron railing surrounding manicured flowers and sculptured trees. I slowly walked over to it, trying not to be upset, and leaned back against the rail, my arms crossed in front of my chest in a defiant stance. What else could I do but wait?

Suddenly, as if out of the blue, a girl walked up to me. She looked like she was alone. It was a girl from my school, a girl I had known only fleetingly.

"Hi Dave," she said, as if she knew me well. I looked around to make sure I was the "Dave" she was addressing. After a moment of panic her name came to me: *Sharon.* I had seen her only occasionally at school and didn't remember having a single class with her in the two years of Junior High. Ironically, I did remember I had sat behind her on the bus to Disneyland that day, catching her momentary glance back at me without remembering the inconspicuous event until that moment. I hadn't said two words to her in my life that I could recall. Yet, Sharon was very cute wearing a purple halter top, a style that was both popular at the time and a little sexy, in a teen sort of way. She wore a pair of white shorts and sandals. I noticed it was an outfit that was accenting those "curves" I was talking about earlier!

Funny how we can recall certain images even decades later.

"Uh, Hi Sharon," I stammered.

"What are you up to?" Sharon asked. She looked so relaxed and comfortable. It was as if she knew I was going to be thrown out of the Matterhorn line and that I would be standing in this very spot.

I didn't want to tell her I got kicked off the Matterhorn so I just said, "I just got here. Some of my friends were already in line for the Matterhorn." I pointed over her shoulder to the entrance of the ride behind her. "I thought I'd wait for them," I added bringing my attention back to Sharon's dark brown eyes, and curves.

Funny how a look, even a look from a thirteen-year-old girl, can issue an emotional tug on the heart strings. I guess I should have asked Sharon why she was all alone talking to me instead of with some of her girlfriends going on rides. Maybe her friends were nearby watching, waiting for some exchanged secret coded sign that signaled her friends she was not going to be joining them. I never knew.

"I was thinking of going on the Matterhorn myself," Sharon said, interrupting my thoughts. She turned and looked behind her just as a bobsled splashed down at the climactic final portion of the ride with riders shrieking in delight. She turned back toward me, taking a little step closer. "You, uh, wouldn't want to go with me would you?" She invaded my 'personal space' and I don't think I've ever felt more conscientious, or enthusiastic. "That is, unless you wanted to wait here for your friends," Sharon said, with what I can only now describe as a pouting lower lip.

Could a thirteen-year-old boy have a heart attack? What friends? Did I come with friends?

"Sssure," I think I stuttered. "That would be fun."

A big smile creased Sharon's lips. She seemed thrilled that I said yes. I was even more thrilled that she asked.

I pushed off the rail and met Sharon's smile.

Somehow, the rest of my day, no, the rest of my life—at least the life I anticipated for that day—was suddenly looking up!

I never found my friends. I never even thought to look for them. The only things I was conscious of were the times Sharon's hand brushed against mine or our hips bumped together while waiting in the Matterhorn line. I remember sitting behind Sharon on the Bobsled, watching her legs when she stepped into the car and then sat in front of me as the ride vehicles were designed for one person in front of the other. I don't know if a thirteen-year old boy designed the vehicles for the Bobsleds, but the moment the car began its climb up the steep incline and Sharon fell back into my chest, I was thinking that the Bobsleds were the best-designed ride in all of Disneyland! My hands were on the handlebars inside the vehicle, which placed them just ahead of Sharon's waist. Eventually, the vehicle began its gravity-aided descent. Every banked turn resulted in Sharon's waist sliding against my arms. Up to that point in my young life, it was as close as I had ever been to holding a girl in my arms!

I knew the Park better than probably most people, having snuck into the place on dozens of occasions, and exploring every single one of its nook's and cranny's. However, being with Sharon, I now saw Disneyland in a completely new light. In fact, that day I don't think I was focused on Disneyland at all. My mind was on this new kind of 'attraction'!

Having Sharon duck her head into my chest on the waterfall of *Pirates of the Caribbean*, going on *People Mover* and sitting side by side, hip to hip—or, cheek to cheek as the case may have been—on the narrow seat, I felt that emotional rush of uncertainty, anticipation, and complete innocent naivety about the opposite sex.

It was on the *Adventure Thru Inner Space* that Sharon first took my hand. *Adventure Thru Inner Space* was the attraction that existed in the location where *Star Tours* is today. Because of the dark, secluded aspect of the ride, *Adventure Thru Inner Space*—or 'Monsanto' as we all called it because it was sponsored by the chemical company of the same name—many young couples made out on the attraction. It became so well known among ride operators for such amorous adventures that it was nicknamed, "Adventure Thru *Intercourse*! At the moment Sharon placed her hand in mine, I tried—probably unsuccessfully—to hide the expression of my surprise mixed with exhilaration that I'm sure was plastered across my face. Luckily, the ride was indeed very dark.

The marquee sign at the entrance of "Adventure Thru Inner Space" at Disneyland before Star Tours took its place. (To us locals back then, it was simply called "MONSANTO".)

Interlocking our fingers was like signing the mortgage agreement for our hearts. I don't remember ever holding hands with anyone except my parents back when I was very young while crossing the street or walking through a parking lot. And the way each of my fingers were curled between Sharon's, this type of holding hands signaled more than just hands being held. It meant we were a 'couple.'

In the darkness of *Adventure Thru Inner Space*, in the privacy of the 'Atommobile, which the clam-shaped ride-vehicles were called for that attraction, I sat in a heightened state of perpetual astonishment and teen bliss. In the glowing phosphorescence of hidden black-lights that illuminated the show elements of the ride, Sharon's skin appeared nearly black against the glowing purple that the white trim of her halter top and white shorts reflected in the blackness of the ride. I remember looking over at her eyes that seemed to float like glowing apparitions over her face.

I was transfixed in the protective darkness, looking at her as she looked at me. Even as I knew she could see me looking directly at her face, the darkness of the ride seemed to remove any self-consciousness that I would normally have felt. Neither Sharon nor I were watching the passing parts of the attraction. The narration was audible to our ears but neither of us was listening.

Adventure Thru Inner Space was a ride that was themed to make guest feel like they were shrinking smaller and smaller as the ride progressed. Snowflakes appeared the size of cars; molecules of H_2O were depicted as giant spheres suspended in air. (One of the first *Hidden Mickey's* was in this attraction where two smaller hydrogen atoms, represented by round balls were poised above a larger, round oxygen atom.) Eventually, the ride narration announced we were becoming even smaller than a molecule, entering the center of the molecule itself. However, sitting there with Sharon, her hand interlinked with mine, I was feeling just the opposite of shrinking.

As we continued to 'shrink', our vehicle now entered the realm of the atom itself, internally manifested by a suspended red 'nucleus' that was pulsating in the middle of a vast room with rounded walls and a curved ceiling. Dots of light projected on the walls danced all around, simulating the so-called electrons orbiting around the atom. At the moment, I was oblivious to the physics that the ride was trying to express or teach. All I could feel was my hand in Sharon's and our eyes on each other.

Like the pulsating red nucleus that I saw in front of us, I felt my heart pounding with teen emotion induced by an influx of male hormones!

Sharon was either far more experienced or far more adventurous than I, because it was there, within the cosmic darkness and pulsating red nucleus that she pressed her lips against mine.

My first kiss; perhaps her first kiss too, I never asked.

We kissed until the narration of the ride said, "Do not panic. We have you back on visual. You will be returning to your normal size." We looked up from our kiss just in time to see a giant eyeball overhead looking down upon us as if we were flattened upon a slide on a microscope stand.

Yep, we were definitely "back on visual." But I was feeling something well beyond "normal"!

Everything seemed to change for me that day. I'm sure each of us goes through those moments of experience that seem to identify major changes in our lives. Mine, like others perhaps, just happened to occur at Disneyland.

That day especially, I concurred with the brochure: Disneyland was indeed "The Happiest Place on Earth"!

Chapter 4
Dancing in the Park

Disneyland seemed to move into a new era in the mid to late 1970s. With the opening of *Space Mountain* in 1977, the Park officially gained a true 'thrill ride' status. While not the intense type of coaster that its neighbor amusement park, Magic Mountain was known for, (Colossus, the Revolution, the Gold Rusher among the coasters Magic Mountain had at that time), Disneyland, however, now had a significant, exhilarating thrill ride.

Between the year Sharon and I shared our first kiss and 1977, I don't remember going to Disneyland, (sneaking in or otherwise), very often. In high school, going to the Park wasn't really considered cool. In fact, for some reason, another friend of mine, also named Mark, and I would drive to Knott's Berry Farm just a few miles away from Disneyland. It was still fairly inexpensive to go into Knott's at that time and it had what was called the "Cloud Nine Ballroom" where live bands played dance music in a room that featured one of the largest dance floors in Orange County. Knott's was catering to the teens more at that period of time. It was a natural place to ask girls to dance then go on some rides or just walk around 'Ghost Town' with them. There was no shortage of dark corners for making out. Knott's had the 'Log ride', which was a nice long attraction with seating similar to that of the Matterhorn cars. One person would sit in front of the first person, making the Log Ride at Knott's, the 'Hug Ride' as the seating invited the back person to wrap their arms around the front rider.

Knott's Berry Farm also had a couple thrill rides: the 'Corkscrew,' the 'Parachute Drop' and one of the best bangs-for-the-buck coasters, 'Montezuma's Revenge. ' It was the first time I had been on a catapult-coaster that shot the riders from 0 to 60 MPH in less than five seconds! Built in 1978, 'Revenge' used the same type of flywheel launch system that were on aircraft carriers used to accelerate fighter jets to flight speeds within short runways.

From 1972 to 1976, my four years in high school, I became a competitive tennis player, setting several school records and becoming fairly well known thanks to my success on our school's tennis team. In addition, I had a steady girlfriend my junior and senior years in high school, which took up my time and sort of eliminated the need to go looking for girls with my friends as we had done a lot of prior to my junior year. Disneyland was an afterthought for many years.

For fun instead, we would head down to the beach, the movies, and Carl's Jr. fast-food restaurants. In the fall, we had football games and dances at school; in the winter we had basketball games and more school dances. The spring was tennis season where my tennis friends and I would play sometimes twelve to sixteen hours of tennis over the weekends. At night, we headed to Loara High School in Anaheim, the only public courts that were lighted.

But the summer of 1976 brought Disneyland back into my life.

After breaking up with my high school girlfriend, my buddy Mark and I would go down to the Disneyland Hotel, this time driving instead of riding bikes. They had a huge grass area in front of the convention rooms and Bonita Tower, a newly expanded wing of hotel rooms that doubled the size of the otel occupancy.

We found that the grass area was perfect for throwing a Frisbee—and being seen throwing a Frisbee! Hotel guests would stop and watch us as we became quite masterful at throwing, catching, and doing tricks with the flying disk. And many times, hotel guests with older teenage daughters frequented the area of grass. Striking up a conversation with a good looking gal was as easy as 'accidently' throwing the Frisbee in their immediate vicinity.

Late one summer afternoon, Mark and I were hanging out at the Hotel, and met two eighteen-year-old girls from Colorado. We ended up having so much fun with the girls, actually acting a lot like kids. We collected all the 'do not disturb' signs from several floors. My 'date' and I were most compatible and enjoyed each other's company, especially in the privacy of the elevators. I lost track of her and don't even remember her name. Yet, I'll never forget that evening or how much fun elevator rides could be.

While many of our friends were dating local girls, we found it just as much fun—if not more fun—meeting girls who were visiting Disneyland from distant locales. There was always so much to talk about with these visitors: where they came from, their schools, things they liked to do, etc. And, for the most part, most of the girls that we met were more than a little excited to meet some 'local boys' that they could tell their friends about when they returned home.

Live bands at Disneyland had always been a staple of the Park from its earliest years. Big bands like Les Brown and His Band of Renown, Lionel Hampton, Count Basie, Harry James and Tommy Dorsey to name just a few, played at the Carnation Plaza to the delight of countless big-band aficionados. In New Orleans Square, trios of musicians played Dixieland Jazz upon the small French Market Stage. Barbershop quartets and a band of five saxophone players filled Main Street USA with classic tunes, knee-slapping melodies, uplifting songs, and ever-present and familiar songs from Disneyland movies.

There was the Golden Horseshoe Saloon, featuring slapstick comedy music. Its world-record number of continuous performances, running over 50,000 shows, made it the longest running stage show in history, a record that will probably never be broken.

I have to admit, however, at the tender age of seventeen or eighteen, for me and my friends, it was the *Tomorrowland Terrace Stage* that always drew our attention. Upon that magical stage, like a rising Phoenix coming up out of its ashes, the *Terrace Stage* rose up from below an intricately designed planter in front of the seating area and dance floor. (This is now where Disneyland does its daily "Jedi Academy" show.) Disneyland had its own bands of professional musicians who played all the hip cover tunes of the late 1970s. From the last days of Disco to the Rock and Roll bands of the '80s, the Tomorrowland Terrace never failed to ignite the area with the most currant sounds of the era.

Another stage was built when *Space Mountain* was constructed. The *Space Stage* at the base of *Space Mountain* was a much more permanent looking stage than the old *Tomorrowland Stage* that had existed in a portion of the land where *Space Mountain* was built. Seating over 1000 guests, the new *Space Stage* was much larger than any other Disneyland stage, allowing much bigger name bands and larger staged performances.

In front of the *Space Stage* was an open area that often became a dance floor. In addition to big-name performers, Disneyland had a house band known as *Papa Do Run Run,* a band that played for an unprecedented fifteen years at the Park, (and still plays concerts all around the country today, more than thirty years later!). The band specialized in playing Beach Boys music as well as songs by Jan and Dean and other classic Rock and Roll hits of the 1960's through the 1980's. (Jan and Dean joined the band for a number of years and a host of celebrities including actor John

Stamos and even Brian Wilson of the *Beach Boys* would occasionally jam with the band at Disneyland!)

What could be more wholesome than dancing to the sounds of the Beach Boys greatest hits? The band encouraged many teens and young adults to come to Disneyland and enjoy the music—and each other. The sense of adventure was instilled nightly as we would meet, dance, and then go on rides in the Park with dates we met each night. In reality, we were living in a fantasy world for a few hours each evening. There were few places that offered the kind of atmosphere that almost magically brought couples together. Sure, there were places to dance all over southern California. And, there were other amusement parks and places to hang out with the opposite sex. But there was only one Disneyland, and the inherent Park atmosphere simply enhanced the dating scene.

In addition to many locals that frequented the Park, as before, I enjoyed the opportunity to meet girls from all over. It was intriguing to learn about them and there was sort of a sense of urgency in some situations. In many cases, the girls visiting the Park were only at Disneyland for one day. When you would meet a person you were interested in, this sense of urgency made you speed up the dating rituals. Holding hands, putting an arm around the other, kissing, and other more romantic expressions were conveyed quickly since both knew that their time together was limited.

A number of us established pen pals with many of the girls we met. Sometimes the exchange of letters would last months and even years. Remember, there was no "Internet" in the 1970's and 1980's! We didn't have Facebook, Twitter, or e-mail to further the relationship. In most cases, at least for those of us who frequented the Park, other dates would supersede most all previous dating interests. I know it might sound cruel or insensitive, however, the facts were, we had only so much time to invest in any girl, and, quite frankly, there was always another Friday or Saturday night at the Park—and a host of potential dates—just a few days away!

It was fun to teach the girls we met new dance moves. And sometimes they taught us some. During the late '70s we were in that transition period where Disco was still active but Rock was becoming more prominent on the radio. With the movie, *Saturday Night Fever*, we were all dressing a little like Tony Manero, the character played by John Travolta. I won't admit to wearing elevator shoes or tight bellbottoms. But I do remember wearing long sleeve shirts, denim vests, and leather jackets.

I think one reason why *Papa Do Run Run* was so popular for the Disney crowd was that it didn't seem to offend those on either side of the Rock/Disco fence. It was Americana music and we loved dancing to familiar songs and watching the bands as they were always very animated and personable. We got to the point that we could almost lip sync the between-song banter among the members of the band.

Enjoying Rides and Shows Vicariously

One thing that really has stayed with me over the years is my enjoyment of showing people things that I am pretty sure they not only were going to enjoy, but things that they otherwise wouldn't have known about. It was sort of reliving my own joy of seeing or doing things for the first time by showing these same things to a date or friends, and vicariously, being able to enjoy such things over and over. I never got tired of seeing Wally Boag and later Dick Hardwick perform their slapstick musical revue at the Golden Horseshoe. My dates always found their funny bone in that theatrical saloon. I enjoyed introducing them to such fun as well as being a part of it.

Among other attractions I enjoyed sharing was *America the Beautiful,* with its 360-degree screens showing breathtaking views of our country. Because it wasn't one of the more visible attractions in the park, most of my dates that were from out of the area enjoyed seeing something that they had not known about or had not planned experiencing. The show was a classic, something that was inspiring for just about anyone, especially if my date had never seen the show before.

And, of course, no date was complete without going into the *Haunted Mansion*! Between the scary setting, humorously animated, for sure, and sitting close to your date in those "Doombuggies," (the ride vehicles that were shaped like clamshells and transported you through the Haunted Mansion), and the darkness of the ride, romance was only a heartbeat—or a scream—away! Even before the actual ride portion, the 'stretching-room' scene always allowed us to protect our dates, putting our arms around them while standing behind them, especially when the lights would go out momentarily and the ceiling revealed a hanging corpse from the rafter. I've memorized the spiel of the narration from countless visits to the attraction.

"Is this room actually stretching? Or is it your imagination? And consider this dismaying observation: this chamber has no window and no doors, which offers you this chilling challenge: to find a way out!"

I'm sure our dates were either amused or annoyed when we would whisper the spiel in their ears! Regardless, we always seemed to have a great time going on Mansion or any of the rides in Disneyland, especially with girls who had never been on or seen those attractions—and even better, if they felt *amorous* on such occasions!

Dancing Waters

Occasionally, we would convince our dates to ride the *Disneyland Monorail* with us to the Disneyland Hotel for a special treat. (Yeah, I know what you're thinking! No, it wasn't that kind of "treat"!) We knew of a unique and one of the best kept secret attractions at the Hotel. Again, it was the opportunity to show a visitor different areas of Disneyland, or in this case, the Disneyland Hotel, that they would never had known about. It was always rewarding for them and for us!

This particular location was called the *"Dancing Waters Show"* held nightly at the Disneyland Hotel. This new kind of show began in May of 1970 at the hotel after several decades of the basic show idea being seen in various locations around the world.

With thousands of feet of pipe, thousands of water nozzles, and dozens of electric pumps and multi-colored lights, the show literally fused water fountains that could be mechanically manipulated to sway with the music or create different angles of the shooting water to form geometric shapes. (Imagine the Dancing Waters as being a precursor to the much larger fountain show at the Bellagio in Las Vegas or Disney's California Adventure recent addition: *The World of Color*.)

Even those who stayed at the hotel often never knew about the unique and entertaining show. *The Dancing Waters* was really one of the first shows in the West that integrated jets of water, lights, and music, and a few years later, "fiber optic" special effects.

The Dancing Waters Show was built in the southwest corner of the hotel grounds, a little out of the way even for people who were visiting the hotel. When the surrounding lights dimmed, the fountains, illuminated by colored lights behind and below the shooting fountains, came to life; all of it choreographed by live, human controllers—not computers. This human manipulation of the lights and fountains made each night's show slightly different. Like any performance, some nights the show seemed more impressive, even for those of us who had seen the show countless times.

The Dancing Waters show changed its name to Fantasy Waters Show in 1992 and the basic show ran from it inauguration in May, 1970 to around 2008 when, after performing two shows nightly for almost forty years, it closed permanently. (You can see clips of the Dancing Waters Show, or, Fantasy Waters Show on YouTube.)

Call it a cheap date, yet taking a girl to the *Dancing Waters Show* was always enjoyable, unexpected in many cases, and always appreciated by those we dated. We didn't have a lot of money as teenagers, nor even a few years later when we were in our first years of college. Even if we did have money to burn, the *Dancing Waters Show* was always such an event for our dates that we probably still would have taken them there. Even after a conventional date for dinner or a movie, a trek to the Dancing Waters Show was almost always enjoyed by our dates and a great finish to any typical night out.

Yet, by 1978, we stopped going to Disneyland for various reasons. It became more difficult to meet women our age there. It wasn't popular for girls in their late teens to frequent Disneyland. For one thing, that age group, male or female, simply stopped doing a lot of things with their families. And this decrease in meeting dates our own age at Disneyland surely contributed to our eventual lack of visiting the Park much after high school.

However, that same year, I again became very involved with Disneyland in a completely new way.

I began working there.

Chapter 5

From Guest to Cast Member

Graduating from Garden Grove High School in 1976, I did what a lot of undecided classmates did: I went to junior college. Unlike a lot of graduating seniors, I didn't have a biting urge to move out of my parent's house or seek college somewhere across the country. I admired those that did venture out on their own. However, sharing a 300-square-foot dorm room with another guy, or trying to figure out how to make rent in a rundown apartment, just didn't have much appeal to me. In addition, I was a young graduate, not even turning eighteen until the July after graduation. I didn't really know what I wanted to do, except for one thing: Play tennis.

While I was a pretty good high school tennis player, I was not nationally ranked. I competed well with many who were and had some good wins against some top-ranked southern California players. Without a national ranking, I had but few options if I wanted to continue to play college tennis. There were three fairly close community colleges in the general area: Orange Coast College, Golden West College, and Santa Ana College. (Santa Ana would be renamed Rancho Santiago Community College a few years later.)

A friend of my father's, Lee Ramirez, head coach at Santa Ana, was the only coach that seemed to show any interest in my playing abilities. By this accord, I went to Santa Ana Community College for the next two years.

My first two years at the JC were basically an extension of high school. Many of my fellow graduates decided, like me, to stay close to home, and attended Santa Ana. Many others went to the other community colleges nearby.

While I enjoyed playing tennis at Santa Ana, and did reasonably well there, I felt like I lacked any individual identity. I dated a few girls there but nothing at all serious. I had a few friends on the tennis team that I hung out with, but we were not close.

It was the summer of 1978, after I had completed my two years of tennis at Santa Ana, when a neighbor said I should interview for a job at Disneyland. Surprisingly, I hadn't given Disneyland much thought during those two previous years. Upon my neighbor's suggestions, I headed down to the employment office near the cast member's entrance. I filled out an application for employment at the Magic Kingdom. However, on the form, I put I would have limited availability on weekends. Because I played a number of tennis tournaments during the summer, I felt it would be tough to work there and compete in tennis.

I returned home to which my neighbor Paul, the one who had suggested I apply, asked if I had gotten an interview yet. I told him no, and he asked about my application. When I told him that I had written I couldn't work all weekends, he almost had a cow.

"You will never get hired if you say you can't work weekends! No, Dave. You drive back down there right now, fill out a new application, and make sure you say you can work every weekend, holiday, and nights." Paul also let me use his name as a referral because at the time, he was working in the costume department at the Park.

I did as he told me. It was another of those moments that would change my life forever.

The Interview

After filling out a new application, I received a call a few days later to come down to 1313 N. Harbor Boulevard, for an in-person interview. The address was, of course, the address for Disneyland, and more specifically, for the administration offices that were next to the employee entrance. (There have been many speculations as to the meaning of the numerical address for Disneyland. One belief is that it was strictly coincidence. However, the thirteenth letter of the alphabet is M. Thus, 1313 could have been Walt Disney's first 'Hidden Mickey': the two letters for that address would be "MM" as in "Mickey Mouse!")

I had no expectations in what job I might land, if I was offered a job. At that time, a job at Disneyland was considered pretty useful on one's résumé. I didn't really see how working at an amusement park was a plus for future employment, but I figured working there would be good for at least a few laughs, if not adding some distinguishing bit of reference to my résumé.

I was pretty relaxed after being called in from the waiting room area, a room that had other young men and women waiting for similar calls for their interviews. Dressed in slacks, shirt and tie, one of the few times I had ever had the urge to wear a tie, I didn't fail to notice the attractive women in the waiting room wearing conservative, but appealing dresses. I believe there was a level of expectation for the interview that was expressed on the application and repeated when I got the call for my interview. Hence, anyone who really DID want to work at Disneyland came dressed to the "T's".

As I left the waiting room, the thought of working in close proximity to any of those pretty young women—and, obviously many others like them—was not soon forgotten.

In the small interview room, I was greeted by another attractive woman, not much older than I. After asking me about my college years, playing tennis, and other work—I had previously worked part time at *Tennisland,* the tennis club affiliated with the Disneyland Hotel a year earlier—she proceeded to ask me a tell-tale question: "Are you comfortable around large groups of people?"

I didn't give her question much thought. I replied quickly, "As a tennis player, you have to be a little, um, cocky." I continued, "I've had to play tennis in front of large crowds at times, so, I guess, I'm very comfortable around any group of people."

The woman sat back in her interview chair. Her subtle grin didn't give anything away. She stood up and said, "I'll be right back."

Her leaving me alone in the room briefly gave me a chance to evaluate the interview to that point and, more specifically, my last answer. *Did I give a good answer or did I give an epic fail?*

The woman returned with a file in her hand. "It looks like we have an opening on the *Davy Crockett Explorer Canoe* ride. Are you familiar with that attraction here at Disneyland?"

In one of those flashes where you see periods of your life pass before your eyes, I thought back to the day my friends and I were sitting on the dock of *Tom Sawyer Island*, the day the canoe passed by us and we marveled at the operator using his paddle to send a stream of water in our direction.

"Yes!" I said perhaps with more enthusiasm than I had displayed during the entire course of the short interview.

"So, I am assuming that might be a position that you would enjoy working?" She asked with a knowing smile creasing her lips.

"Sure. I think that would be terrific!"

She held her hand out to me. "Congratulations, David. You are hired."

Disneyland University

A couple days later, I attended a mandatory four-day Disneyland training period. A portion of this training was called the *Disneyland University*. The first two days were extensive eight-hour orientations, specifically focusing on what it means to be working at Disneyland. This included an informative history of Walt Disney followed by the "Disney Way," a philosophy of the Park in which we learned people visiting the Park are called "Guests" not tourists and those of us working at Disneyland were "Cast Members" not employees. Being in the Park where the guests were was called 'On Stage' while working behind the scenes was called 'Backstage.' Also described was the appearance Disneyland demanded of its cast members: Men: hair had to be above the collar and above the ears; no facial hair at all. Women could only wear inconspicuous make up, one non-dangling earring in each ear, and hair neatly groomed.

Like the interview a few days earlier, all the guys wore ties and girls wore dresses for this orientation. There were at least thirty of us in our orientation training group. You could already see the gears turning. In-between listening to the information being given, guys and girls were subtly—and not so subtly—screening the other sex for possible encounters at some point. It was even more interesting when we broke into smaller groups of cast members who would indeed be working in the same area of the Park.

We were given an entire tour of the backstage areas of Disneyland; from the storage warehouses—they never throw ANYTHING away!—to where they shoot the fireworks off, from the horse stables to a tour beneath the *Pirates of the Caribbean* ride, where one of the two employee cafeterias was located. We were given a crash course in everything Disney and everything Disneyland!

The next two days were spent being trained at our individual attractions or job locations in the Park. Being hired to work the *Davy Crockett Explorer Canoes* ride, I reported to the attraction at the predetermined time to meet with Art, the foreman on the ride who was going to be my trainer. In reality, I was trained by a number of experienced RO's, (Ride Operators), in addition to Art.

The first thing taught was steering a two-ton canoe, (which each weighted when filled with eighteen people), around Tom Sawyer Island along the *Rivers Of America*. That was the official name of the body of water that surrounded Tom Sawyer Island. Using a five-and-a-half foot long paddle like a rudder, I was surprised to see how easy it was to maneuver the thirty-five foot long canoe around the river. It was a little more difficult to make turns when the canoe was moving slowly, as in when hardly anyone was paddling, which was most of the time when you had guests responsible for the locomotion of the canoe. However, when given a good group of paddling guests, or, especially during canoe races, which I'll talk about later, you could turn the long, pointed bow of the canoe, on a dime.

Above, a rear steerer uses his paddle to make a right turn. By pulling in with the left hand, the paddle angles to the right acting like a rudder, pushing the back of the canoe to the left and the front of the canoe will go to the right.

Below, a rear steerer reaches out on the left side of the canoe and pulls in to make the canoe go to the right. This move requires more strength than using the paddle against the canoe rail as in the photograph above.

Unlike the typical perception of the attraction, the canoes were not on a track and there was no motor. The sole means of getting the canoe to move was left up to the riders using their three and four-foot paddles, and, of course, the two ride operators, one in front and one in the rear. The rear operator was also responsible for steering as with any canoe. The front operator, known as the front steerer was ultimately responsible to encourage the guests to paddle after a short dissertation on how to hold the paddle and then use it to propel the canoe forward. If necessary, the front steerer could also be involved in helping steer the canoe. Occasionally, if the front steerer was with a rookie rear steerer, he would have to make corrections if the rear steerer made the wrong turn. For some novice RO's on the canoes, many came to the attraction with little—if any—working experience with any watercraft, to understand the working relationship of a rudder for directional control. For example, with the five-and-a-half foot-long paddle used to steer the Disneyland canoes, the rear steerer would have to pull the handle of the paddle to the left to turn the canoe to the right when the paddle was on the right side of the canoe. On a number of occasions, beginning canoe operators would get mixed up and turn the canoe the wrong way and the front steerer would have to make a quick correction, which would prompt him to stand and frown at the rookie after correcting the turn.

Using the gunwales of the side of the canoe for leverage, you would use one hand to act as a yoke of holding the paddle against the canoe, while the hand on the top of the paddle could pull in to make a turn. To make turns to the opposite direction, the steerer would either switch to the other side of the canoe and repeat the action, or, a little more difficult and strength dependent, the steerer could lean out away from the canoe, reaching out with the paddle, and pull in to make the canoe go in the other direction. This method was not as effective a way to make the canoe turn but could be used to make minor course corrections as needed.

Probably the hardest part of working the canoes was for ride operators to help coordinate the sixteen or so guests in each canoe to paddle in unison. (There were two guests to each of the eight available seats. There were also a single seat behind the front steerer and another single seat in front of the rear steerer.) If one person stopped or slowed down their paddling stroke, the person behind them—and subsequently, those further behind—would have to be paying attention so as to not reach forward for a stroke and hit the paddle in front of them. (This usually caused someone to get wet.) And, considering the attraction was ultimately a ride for sightseeing the areas along the river, few guest paid much attention to the task of paddling the canoe as a team. If the guests hardly paddled, even after some encouragement from the front steerer, one or both of the RO's would ultimately have to paddle a lot more to get the canoe around the river.

Unless the ride operators had to get a canoe around the river fast, as in the last canoe out for the day before closing the ride at dusk, each trip was usually done at a leisurely pace by both the guests and the operators. The real exception was when the *Mark Twain* or the *Columbia* sailing ship, (the two largest crafts on the river), approached a canoe. Luckily, between the front and rear steerers in the canoe, they alone could propel the canoe faster than either big ship.

It was always fun to pull the canoe out in front of the *Mark Twain* or the *Columbia*, with a canoe load of guests. After giving a quick demonstration on how to use the paddle, the front steerer would offer a little added encouragement:

"If any of you would like some incentive to paddle faster, just look behind the canoe... That is the Mark Twain, [or Columbia], which weighs about 150 tons, and it doesn't stop very quickly."

The look on the faces of the guests as they spied the massive river boat or sailing ship bearing down on them was always priceless. It didn't take a second prodding by the ride operator to encourage them to paddle faster. However, in reality, the two ride operators could move the canoe fast enough to outrun either big ship.

Confidence Came Quickly

Working the canoes brought a level of confidence in most all who worked the ride. Having the freedom to steer the canoe almost anywhere around the river, the fun of making the guests laugh, and getting a terrific upper body workout were merits enough. Wearing one of the coolest outfits in the Park was another perk.

Our brown pants looked a little like leather, even though they were made of very comfortable cotton. The outer seam on the pants had fringe running down the leg that also resembled leather. Our shirts were also very comfortable. Open at the collar with a draw string, the shirts were a pale yellow, almost a mustard color, which went well with the pants. Unlike many attraction hosts' costumes within the Park—most of which were made of polyester for durability, and certainly of questionable style—the canoe costume was not only comfortable, but relatively attractive too. Wearing leather moccasins on bare feet was another plus, especially during the hot, summer afternoons working in the Park. Taking off our moccasins while sitting in the back of the canoe steering, and slipping your feet in the water over the side of the canoe, was always relaxing. Since you were in the back of the canoe during the trip, and about half the trip was along the uninhabited sides of Tom Sawyer Island and the mainland areas, no one could see what you were doing in the back of the canoe.

Completing the outfit was a simulated coonskin cap with a dangling tail. The hat was open on the top, so it was more like wearing a wool visor instead of a hat, and the tail would hang down in the back, occasionally becoming an annoyance if it swung over your shoulder and landed against the side of your face.

It was within a few days after my training that I also discovered another benefit of working the canoes: Girls.

As I soon realized, the canoe ride operators were sometimes considered the "rock stars" of the Park.

Canoe History

Opened in 1956, the year after Disneyland itself opened, the *Davy Crockett Explorer Canoes* first operated as the *Indian War Canoes*, not a very "politically correct" title by today's standards! It was located in the Indian Village, an extended 'land' from Frontierland. Later, after Disneyland closed the Indian Village in 1971, the canoes were closed, then reopened later that year as well as being renamed *The Davy Crockett Explorer Canoes*. The ride became part of what was then called Bear Country the next year. The two areas, New Orleans Square and Bear Country, were tied together for employees working the attractions in each. If you worked in one of the two areas, you could be trained to work on attractions in the other area as well. The loading dock and queue for the Canoes was located where it is today, near the lower patio of the Hungry Bear Restaurant. Later, in 1989, the area *Bear Country* was renamed *Critter Country* after the Country Bear Jamboree attraction was removed and Splash Mountain was built.

Originally, the canoe used real American Indian guides. When ticket books were used, the ride was a surprising "D" Ticket attraction, a ticket just below the famous "E" Ticket. Considering the canoes were free-floating and had no other means of propulsion than the guides and the guests paddling, I always found it amusing that people were willing to pay the second highest priced ticket to actually 'work!'

If I thought meeting friends and women in the Park as a guest was fun and easy, I was in for a pleasant surprise when I started working at Disneyland.

The first thing you discover as a cast member is that you are literally surrounded by young, fun-loving, and for the most part, attractive fellow cast members. There are even a few 'lifers,' men and women in their late 30s, 40s, and 50s who had worked in the Park for years, if not decades. I often considered Disneyland an extension of high school, only everyone was a lot more mature and instead of a thousand fellow students, Disneyland had about eight-thousand fellow cast members!

There is a saying while working at Disneyland: "If you can't get a date working at Disneyland, you CAN'T get a date." Needless to say, it was 'dating heaven' working at Disneyland!

Many relationships were created through working at the Park. A lot of future marriages were forged by cast members working together or meeting through other Disney social channels. There was no shortage of parties, cast member activities, both sponsored by Disney and not, and simple get-togethers at local restaurants, bars, nightclubs, after work.

Cast Activities

In the late seventies and early eighties, during my six years working at Disneyland, there was a cast member service called the DRC: *Disneyland Recreation Club*. Among the many events sponsored and organized by Disneyland were the summer slow-pitch softball leagues. These featured hundreds of teams from all areas of the Park. Teams consisted of men's, women's, and mixed teams. Some played for the social aspect, some for competition and exercise, and others for bragging rights within certain areas of the Park. Games were played throughout Anaheim at public fields, usually in the evenings, which meant players would have to juggle shifts for their team. It was common to see a deluge of shift change requests issued at the beginning of each week so that players could play on their team.

Canoe Racing

One of the most unique and popular recreational events held annually was the Disneyland Employee Canoe Races held during the early morning hours throughout late June and July. They are still being held annually. Back in the late 1970s, over 1500 cast members participated in the ten-person teams. And, like softball, groups of cast members formed men's, women's, and mixed canoe teams.

The advantage of canoe racing for many, unlike softball, volleyball, bowling, and all the other cast activities, was that the races were held in the early morning hours before the Park opened, usually starting at five am and ending before eight am. This was great for most people since it seldom interfered with their work schedule. However, the down side was the great number of cast members who partied a lot of nights. They found it very difficult to get up that early, and then paddle a canoe to the point of exhaustion, or worse, throwing-up! And there were those who worked swing shifts, either in maintenance, janitorial, or landscaping. Many of those cast members would get off at 3am, head to the nearby Denny's Restaurant for a post-shift breakfast and then return to the employee parking lot where they would sleep in their cars until it was time for their canoe team to race. Needless to say, this was a sport more for the younger cast members! (Although, there were many old-timers who still raced and enjoyed the camaraderie the races offered.)

Each canoe team had two weeks to practice after attending the mandatory Steering Clinic where some of the canoe ride operators volunteered to teach novice steerers how to guide their team's canoe. In all reality, almost no team could compete without a canoe ride operator as their rear steerer, or, at the very least, someone in the back who had some working knowledge and experience piloting a canoe.

Team Practice and Steering Clinic: Author David Smith turning the canoe around while his women's team paddles.

The Steering Clinic was made up of canoe ride operators. We would work with each team's rear steerer and teach them how to maneuver effectively and avoid crashing a fast-moving canoe into something that wasn't moving—which resulted in an automatic disqualification. At the end of the two week clinic, Gail, our incredible Cast Activities Director, would take all the steering clinic volunteers and their dates out to the *Warehouse*, an upscale, steak and seafood restaurant in Newport Beach as a "thank you" for our services. It was one of those events that we all looked forward to doing each summer.

"Bad News Canoes"

It was my second summer, in 1979, that I decided to form my own canoe team. I had been hired too late to be involved in the races my first summer working. By my second summer, not only had I learned all about the races, I had heard about the legendary team of Lifeguards from the Disneyland Hotel who had won the men's division many years in a row. These guys were physically prime specimens, chiseled and cut men, who must have worked out in the gym every moment they were not watching the Disneyland Hotel guests frolicking in the pools. The team from the Hotel was named "**Engulf and Devour.**" No other men's team had even come close to beating them in the last five years.

I decided to form a canoe team called the **Bad News Canoes**. After working the canoe ride the previous season, I realized that using the four-foot long paddles, it was not how strong you were, it was how fast you could pull the paddle through the water countering the friction that the weight of the canoe possessed when moving that counted. Stamina and limiting the weight in the canoe seemed to me to be more important that brute strength.

Bad News Canoes getting ready to race!

Having played tennis as well as having coached high school tennis alongside my nationally recognized tennis coach/father, Bruce Smith, I knew a lot about motivation, organization, and team strategy. Thus, I sought out a team of guys to form a men's team that met three specific qualifications: 1) they worked the canoe ride, 2) were the smallest canoe ride operators I could find, and 3) and were rookies.

My strategy was this: The smaller guys would weigh less than bulky, big guys creating a greater strength-to-weight ratio. Because the 4 foot paddles used in the races were relatively small, a 90 pound weakling could theoretically pull the paddle through the water just as fast as a guy who could bench press 400 pounds! I wanted guys who worked the canoe ride so they could basically get a workout everyday on the muscles and stamina needed to paddle the canoe steady for the four minutes or so that it took to get around Tom Sawyer Island during the race. I also wanted new guys so they had no previous understanding of the dynasty the Hotel lifeguards had created. I believed psychologically, if my guys knew that *Engulf and Devour* had dominated the races as they had, that my team would be more intimidated by that one fact.

For the canoe races, two weeks of practice were followed by two weeks of qualifying timed races. There were upwards of well over one hundred total teams within the three divisions: Men's, Mixed, and Women's. After the first week, the top twelve teams in each division went on to the second week. The end of the second week produced the top four teams who would race in the finals. The next group of four teams that didn't make the finals would race the day before the finals in a "Sprint Championship," a head-to-head—or canoe-to-canoe—sprint of about three hundred yards starting near the raft dock and ending at the finish line at the canoe dock.

All through the races, my team, *Bad News Canoes* held a slight edge. During the last qualifying times, we held about a two second advantage over *Engulf and Devour* as well as another fast team, *Entertainment I*, (a team made up of the sound, lighting, and electrical crew that ran the entertainment stages in the park). One other team from the Parking Lot filled out the final four and the stage was set for the annual Canoe Race Championships.

Since *Bad News Canoes* had the fastest time going into the finals, we went out last. Much like certain Olympic events, the early teams out had a slight advantage because there usually was no breeze at that hour to make the water surface ripple to add friction along the sides of the canoe as it plied the water. Ironically, the *Entertainment I* team and the team of *Engulf and Devour* had an exact tie for the lead on the final day, both posting a time of four minutes, eleven seconds, and eight-tenths of a second. (4:11.8)

David Smith shouts out the cadence of paddling and practicing the switches for his women's canoe team

These were very competitive races with hundreds of fans watching. It was the one day that Disneyland allowed anyone into the Park for free to watch the races! There were television cameras from one of the local stations and newspaper reporters and photographers. The official timing system was very sophisticated; a laser start and finish line marker was used to start and stop the clock. Four hand-held stop watches were used to confirm the official times. A large digital clock was mounted on Tom Sawyer Island across from the canoe dock where fans at Hungry Bear Restaurant could easily see each team's time as they raced.

My team had been backstage behind Hungry Bear Restaurant stretching out and trying to stay calm. When we jogged out to the staging area to get in the canoe for our final run, we heard that there was a tie for first place. Discussions were being made by the officials to determine how a tie would be handled since there had never been a tie in the fifteen year history of the races. No one seemed to be giving us much thought even as we had led all weeks with the fastest time. It was as if no believed a bunch of rookie canoe racers, (all who looked like they were little kids compared to the size of our opposing canoe teams), could seriously win. Another reason no one thought we would win was because the tied times of *Engulf and Devour* and *Entertainment I* was faster than any times previously posted by us in the weeks leading up to the final.

Under the buzz of the crowd talking about the two teams tied for the lead, my team methodically got into our canoe, each member of my team taking their familiar places. Mine was in the third seat from the front. Karl, our only experienced member, was our rear steerer and one of the smallest guys on the team. As captain, I ran my team through practice 'switches,' the precise way the entire team would switch sides to paddle on so their arms would not give out trying to paddle the entire time on one side. Each member sat on the opposite side of the canoe from the teammate ahead of him. The switches had to be perfect without a single person missing their slide across the narrow canoe seat, or falling off the seat, and without missing a beat. If the paddling slowed down for even a half second, the canoe would sit down into the water, and decelerate considerably. Also, the switch was done with such precision that there would be minimal rocking of the canoe, another situation that would slow the canoe.

After moving our canoe into the river and lining up the nose of the canoe with the laser beam starting line, each of our members assumed their starting position, paddles up over the water; bodies leaned forward and out over the rail to make the initial pull back when the starting pistol would fire.

Unlike most teams, I had a strategy to start with deeper and slower, initial strokes, instead of a bunch of really fast, quick strokes that was the standard for the teams over the years. I had figured that the four-foot paddles were so small relative to the weight of the canoe that pulling them through fast was like a sprint car spinning his tires at a drag race start, instead of the tires gripping the pavement. I taught our guys to go much deeper and pull with a deliberate action that increased with speed with each successive pulls. Karl, our rear steerer would count out the start, building up our speed with each count of the strokes until we hit ten, at which point we had gotten our speed up very, very fast. At this point we would slow into a methodical cadence to be maintained for the rest of the race.

All of us could not wait for each of the switches as the paddling was the equivalent of sprinting a hundred yards, except using our arms instead of our legs. The pain from muscle fatigue of one arm pulling the paddle through the water was enormous. The switch brought fresh arms as we slid over to opposite sides of the canoe from where each of us had been paddling. This freshness, of course, would only last about twenty seconds before the fatigue built up on this arm and our muscles would be screaming for another switch.

The trip around Tom Sawyer Island was five-eighths of a mile, but in the canoe races it felt more like ten miles. And, knowing that between a half second to two or three seconds usually separated first from fourth place in the races, there was a ton of pressure on Karl, our rear steerer, to make the turns around the Island perfect. Too wide, we would lose precious time; too close to the Island and brushing against the reeds, one side of the canoe wouldn't be able to paddle for a moment. You could count your team out if that happened.

As we came around the final turn called the "Stage Turn," people were lined up on the river wall in front of *Pirates of the*

Caribbean and the *Haunted Mansion*, cheering us on. I remember hearing someone yell, "You guys are a half second behind!"

Karl yelled at us to dig in, and we did. However, I didn't know if all these little guys had enough strength left to make up that time in the last three hundred yards.

There was so much screaming by the fans as we approached the finish line. The spectators could see the clock on the Island posting our time as we came across. However, we were so exhausted that all we could hear was the compression of our hearts pounding in our chests with each last pull of our paddles. As we passed under the finish line banner, we all just collapsed, our lungs heaving, trying to recapture some oxygen.

I glanced over to the Island to see our time; the digital clock only showed the minutes and seconds...not the tenths of a second. The time read: 4:11...four minutes, eleven seconds; the same minutes and seconds that *Engulf and Devour* had as their tied time with *Entertainment I*. Confused, we dragged our paddles in the water to slow the canoe down. There we sat, dead in the water in front of hundreds of spectators looking down at us from the Hungry Bear Restaurant patios and the canoe dock. The place went dead silent. No one knew what our official time was yet. We were not even sure if the clock on the Island was even accurate. We might have a time that was even worse than the 4:11 that was posted there.

My team waited in the canoe, our arms rubber and our hearts trying to catch up; our bodies spent. All we could do was lean forward trying to catch our breath and not puke in front of anyone, all the while waiting for the announcement of our time.

Finally, over the loud speakers the time was called out:

"Time for Bad News Canoes: Four minutes, eleven seconds and...."

We held our breath not wanting to hear any number larger than "Eight tenths". All of Disneyland was dead quiet as everyone waited.

Finally, the announcement of the tenths of a second:

"Four tenths."

The crowd went wild. We had beaten *Engulf and Devour* as well as *Entertainment I* by a mere four tenths of a second.

Suddenly, all our fatigue was lost. Euphorically, all the members of my team dove into the water, thankfully caught on film by the *Register Newspaper*.

Traditional Sinking of the Canoes by the victorious men's, women's, and mixed canoe teams after the finals of the Disneyland Canoe Races. Center left, David Smith signals his team's first-place finish before going down with the canoe!

We took the traditional victory lap along with the women's winners and the mixed winners. The lap that took about thirty minutes to complete since we did little paddling and just splashed each other's canoe as we inched around Tom Sawyer Island. Upon our return to the canoe dock, we proceeded to sink each of the canoes! Well, they can't sink...but we did fill them completely full of water and celebrated in the middle of the River with the mixed and women's teams! After the celebration which went on for another half hour, we needed to pump the water out of the canoes. Hey, we still had to open Disneyland in less than an hour! We quickly got the canoes pumped and then all the teams attended an awards celebration on the upper deck of Hungry Bear Restaurant.

My team of rookie canoe operators, some who had only worked in the Park for a month, were each now pseudo celebrities, at least among those who followed the canoe racing at Disneyland. It was an event that certainly capped off the summer for all of us. Of course, within a week, it had all died down and we went back to having fun both inside and outside Disneyland.

Ironically, it would be the final year that *Engulf and Devour* ever competed as a team.

"Enter Xenon", David Smith's winning women's team just after receiving their awards as the Sprint Race Champions!

Sprint Races

For fun, I always formed a women's canoe team. In addition to having ten women on a team with me as their male captain, it was really fun for both my men's and women's teams to go out together for an annual pre-race dinner at the Spaghetti Factory in Newport Beach.

I also always hosted at least one huge party at my house during the summer, mostly for the cast members in my area of the Park. This party grew to be well over 100 cast members but the parties never got out of hand, thankfully!

My women's canoe team was never taken as seriously as the men's teams. So, I just had fun with the girls, and we usually finished in the top four or top eight every year. The same year my men's team won, my women's team qualified for the sprint races. My team that year was a team named after a sexy pinball machine called, "Enter Xenon." The girls wore funny wigs, fishnet stockings, and even dressed *me* up!

In our first heat, we were to race against a serious looking group of very masculine-looking women from janitorial.

In the Sprint Races, the race was a head to head sprint with each winning team moving on to a final heat for the championship. I didn't have a lot of expectations against this very strong-looking team in the first round.

The rule for the rear steerer was that we could not paddle, only steer the canoe to keep it straight toward the finish line.

My team, not surprisingly, were picked because they were fun and very cute, not necessarily for their athleticism. (Although, they were not bad in the athletic department either!) However, like my men's team, the girls I picked were smaller than the girls on some of the other teams. And the lack of size in the canoe makes a world of difference, especially when you are only racing for three-hundred yards.

Well, my girls beat not only the team of "studs," (nosing them by a mere three inches in the head-to-head race), we went on and won the Sprint Championship race as well!

Tranquil Early Mornings

The Canoe Races offered a few of us a unique opportunity that only a handful of cast members got to experience.

As officials for the canoe races or Steering Clinic volunteers, some of us helped out by getting to the Canoe dock very early, assisting in setting up for either the steering clinic or the races themselves.

Canoe Race Officials on the bow of the Mark Twain. 1983

Coming into Disneyland just as the sun was coming up over the horizon, the Park nearly devoid of human life, you got to walk through the empty streets and themed areas as if you were the only person alive. Like a movie set, the Park lacked life when there was nothing going on. It was a lot like walking through a real-life ghost town.

Sometimes I walked into the Park alone, other times in groups or pairs. Since we didn't have to change into our costumes for the races, I would walk directly through to the hub, through the cast member's entrance to the Park between *Main Street USA* and the entrance to *Tomorrowland*. The moment you stepped out onto *Main Street*, you often could feel the presence of Walt Disney in some ethereal way. Perhaps it was the vacancy of the Park at five in the morning. Or, perhaps it was the silence that pervaded the Park like a heavy blanket. It was a silence that we knew would be shattered in a few hours by tens of thousands of guests and all the operational aspects of the Park.

There usually was one sound heard as you crossed the north hub of *Main Street* and entered either Frontierland or

Adventureland: The recorded singing coming from Snow White's wishing well to the right of *Sleeping Beauty's Castle* was usually always left on. The faint, reverberated sound of Snow White, singing, "I'm wishing" could only be heard from such a distance away when it was dead quiet in the Park.

The Snow White grotto, a tranquil location even when the Park is open to the public, features beautiful sculpted figures of Snow White and the Seven Dwarfs. The exquisite statues were mysteriously donated to the Park from someone in Italy in 1961. Through the use of forced perspective, Snow White appears to be larger than the dwarfs that surround her, even though she was mistakenly carved at the same height.

Hearing Snow White's airy falsetto voice in the heavy morning air always heightened the feeling of Walt's presence for me. Especially on rare mornings when there was a mist or fog hanging in the air, the sound of Snow White's voice would carry an even more eerie quality to the early morning experience.

For those who knew about Walt Disney's apartment on Main Street near the Park Entrance over the Disneyland Fire Station, one could experience an added sense of Disney Magic especially in the early morning hours.

When Walt Disney was alive, a lamp in his apartment would be turned on. When he was gone, the apartment was dark. After Walt died, the lamp in the center window above the Fire Station continues to be left on 365 days a year in honor of Walt Disney's spirit, still alive in the Park even decades after his death.

There have been many sightings of shadows moving in the apartment. Upon inspections of the apartment, never once has there been anything found to explain the sightings.

The presence of Walt Disney has been felt by many a cast member.

Chapter 6

Same Park, Different Day;

Canoes

Working at Disneyland offered most all cast members a variety of situations nearly every day. Some could be expected, like the strange questions we would be asked, daily, by guests: "What time is the three o'clock parade?" or, "Where is Magic Mountain?" Some things could never be anticipated.

Certainly, when you put twenty to fifty thousand people in a Park such as Disneyland, you get a pretty good sampling of a cross section of humanity. From the brain-dead to the people determined to have a bad day; from people doing the bizarre to bizarre things happening to innocent people, we could almost expect the unexpected on a daily basis while at work in the Happiest Place on Earth.

A slew of very funny and interesting stories about cast members and guests can be read in the book, ***Mouse Tales; A Behind-The-Ears Look at Disneyland*** by David Koenig. However, there are a number of stories that have not been told in any book prior to this one. And, I'm sure, there are countless more stories by other cast members that I'm certainly not aware of.

During my six years working at Disneyland, I was trained on four attractions: *Canoes, Pirates of the Caribbean, Keel Boats,* and the *Monorail.* Each ride had its own set of situations that offered up humor, intrigue, and even romance!

Canoes

As I've described, the first ride I was trained on was the Davy Crockett Explorer Canoes attraction. The canoes offered up some interesting situations both from the interaction with fellow workers as well as interesting things that guests did.

Canoe Operations

Working the canoe dock was basically herding a specific number of guests into one of three queue areas, each one holding enough people to fill one canoe. You could put as many as sixteen guests in one canoe plus the two ride operators. Behind the front steerer and in front of the rear steerer, there was one seat which we liked to keep empty but could put a single passenger in if needed. All the seats in-between these were wide enough to seat two adults, assuming they had average sized rear ends. While the seats were wide enough to seat two people, the seats themselves, slender wooden slats, really, were very narrow and occasionally, people would miss-judge the width of the seat as they tried to sit and slip off the back, landing in a somewhat embarrassing position. In addition, the seats were very low, so people with stiff knees or bad backs always had difficulty getting down to the seat. If ever an attraction should have a sign: "Not recommended for pregnant people and people with bad backs!" the Canoes certainly should have qualified. Add to these rather uncomfortable seats the fact that you really did have to paddle to make the canoe go, the ride for all practical purposes, was really work!

Typically, people would inadvertently splash someone either in front of them or behind them. We always let them keep all the water that each person collected while on the ride! On hot, summer days, a splash could be actually refreshing—if not a little shocking at first, depending on the amount of water received and if you had seen it coming or not. Of course, some women would get splashed on their shirts creating a somewhat "revealing" nature depending on their tops and what they wore—or didn't wear—underneath!

The canoes would usually come in with some water on the sides of the seats from a previous trip. Occasionally, someone getting ready to sit on the seat would shout, "Hey, my seat is wet."

With deadpan wit, our typical response was, "As soon as you sit down, it will dry up."

Most people got the joke, but many would take the remark as if there was some Disney magic that would remove the water before their clothes absorbed it.

Reminding people to keep their hands inside the canoe until it got out of the dock was as morbid as it was funny. Usually our spiel would be something like, "Please keep your hands and fingers inside the canoe until we leave the dock, unless you want to carry them home in a bag."

People often did exactly as they were told on every ride without even giving the advice any conscious thought. One such example of this was when we had the canoe loaded and the two RO's would start pulling the ropes attached to the front and the back of the canoe. The front guy, obviously straining to get the now fully loaded and very heavy canoe moving through the narrow loading dock would ask the crew of guests, "Could everyone lean forward a little to help us out?"

Every guest would lean forward as if somehow that would make pulling the canoe move faster. After a few seconds, the RO would then deadpan, "No, really, it helps cut down air friction."

Once we pull out into the river, the RO in the front of the canoe would give a short spiel instructing the crew on how to paddle and then sit down in front and start paddling with the guests. Depending on the personality of the front guide, the make-up of the guests in the canoe, or how we felt on any given day, the ride operator in the front of the canoe might stand up and give periodic spiels along the trip. Most of us enjoyed giving impromptu spiels as many of us felt the guest sort of expected some sort of narration, as they would get on the other boats that circumnavigated Tom Sawyer Island. And, because the Jungle Cruise attraction sort of set the bar for funny spiels, people seemed to expect the same while on the canoes. Because we didn't have a specific SOP spiel, (a "Standard Operating Procedure" spiel Disneyland scripted for a particular attraction that offered spiels as part of the ride), canoe operators were able to mostly adlib around the River. Jokes were handed down over the years and sometimes new jokes were thought up. Working with different canoe partners allowed each RO a chance to hear other spiels and different jokes. Some guys working the ride had great timing and delivery, even to the point of cracking up not just the guests, but his partner in the back of the canoe as well. However, occasionally, some operators never developed a sense of humor or lacked the personality to evoke such humor. Being paired with someone like that usually made for a long day. Luckily, there were few RO's who resembled this description!

Some of our jokes were about paddling the canoe and others were about the scenes along the river. One impromptu spiel occurred when we had a lot of women on the ride:

"Paddling is good exercise: for you men, it builds up your biceps, shoulders, and chests. For you women, it builds up your biceps, shoulders, and egos."

As I had seen as a youngster while sitting on one of the piers on _Tom Sawyer Island_, canoe ride operators learned to smack the water with their paddles. Done right, this move could produce a perfect spray of water as far as thirty feet. It was quite a skill to be able to not only direct the spray of water in a particular direction, but to control the length of the spray based on how hard you brought the paddle down against the water.

We got to the point where we could literally hit a tin can from twenty-five feet away. It was fun to impress guests on the Island with a spray that would land right at their feet. Girls seemed to love it when we did it in their direction, perhaps one of the reasons so many girls often found their way to the canoe dock at the time we shut the ride down at dusk!

Faced with an entire canoe-load of guests who didn't speak a word of English, giving the instructions on how to paddle became a game of charades for the front RO. Miming how to hold the paddle, how to use the paddle, and attempting to point things out was often amusing.

One of the challenging aspects we created was to see how fast we could get the canoe moving in the dock by pulling the ropes and running along the dock as we launched a canoe. We would sometimes need to do this as the Mark Twain or the Columbia Sailing Ship was coming up the river near the canoe dock. No one liked being caught behind either big ship since they moved very slowly; if you didn't get out in front of them, it would become nearly a 20 minute trip.

Because the canoe dock ended abruptly, the front RO would have to jump in while on the run and the rear RO had to pull in on the rope at the last second to get the canoe pointed in the right direction and then jump in. Occasionally, an RO would misjudge the speed or trip trying to jump into the canoe and fall into the river at the end of the dock. Unfortunately for the befallen cast member, it was also right in front of the people eating on the lower tier of Hungry Bear Restaurant, which usually resulted in clapping and a lot of laughter at the expense of the embarrassed and very wet RO.

Steering the canoes was not difficult. However, there were two areas of each trip that could be a little challenging:

The Rapids: This is a stretch of large rocks that jut out along the side of the river near the back side of Tom Sawyer Island. There was a gap between the land and the line of rocks, large enough for the canoes to go through. In fact, this was part of the ride that the canoes were supposed to go through, unless two canoes were approaching the entrance at the same time, where one would have to go around the rapids. The term 'rapids' was coined because there were small underwater jets that moved water around the rocks, simulating rapids. However, the amount of water moved was so small that we all made fun of it by saying, "Oh, my, we are entering the treacherous Canoe Rapids. Look at the white water," at which point we would playfully splash a little water with our paddle upon the rocks simulating the treacherous white water.

On very rare occasions, a duck might stick its head in the intake portion of the jets that produced the 'white water'. The suction would pull the duck into the jet and drown it; not exactly a pleasant sight for anyone! Luckily, when it did happen, the first canoe out would inform Maintenance who would quickly come out and remove the dead duck before any other guests could witness the duck's demise! Years later, I had heard that Disneyland placed metal grates over the intake portion of the jets.

However, the Rapids will forever have another meaning to me as the time I was involved with finding something else dead in the Rapids: a person. It would be the following year when I was working on Keel Boats. I will share the details of that discovery in the next chapter.

Raft Crossing: The second area that could be challenging for a canoe steerer was the approach to the *Tom Sawyer Island Raft's* crossing zone. Typically, the raft driver on the mainland side, the area on the river between *Pirates of the Caribbean* and the

Haunted Mansion, would look out toward the *Mark Twain* landing, the area in front of Frontierland. This is where the raft driver would first be able to see if any river craft were approaching, such as the canoes, Keel Boats, Mark Twain, or the Columbia. Upon entering the area where the rafts normally cross, any canoe's front steerer would look back behind him and see how many canoes were coming around the stage turn with him, if any. (The stage turn was the hard right-turn around the stage that is built at the edge of the Island for the nighttime show, "Fantasmic!" This turn was just before the area that the Tom Sawyer Island Rafts would cross.) The ride operator would look for the attention of the Raft Driver across the river at the Tom Sawyer Island dock and signal with his fingers how many canoes were coming around the stage turn. Because the raft driver on the Island side was completely blind to what was coming around the stage turn in the river there, he would, in turn, receive a signal from the other Raft Driver on the mainland side of first how many canoes, or big ships were coming, and then receive a hand signal to come across.

Occasionally, if you had a fast canoe, you would come around the stage turn so fast that the rafts were already crossing in front of your canoe. That situation was where experienced steerers, both in the front and in the back of the canoe, could be ever so helpful...and inexperienced steerers would panic! The steerer had to anticipate where the rafts would be moving and judge how to miss both the one coming across from the Island and the other moving across from the mainland side. It was like the movie *Matrix* where a bullet had to be dodged by several moving people.

I've seen canoes actually hit one of the rafts head on, which usually doesn't result in anyone getting hurt but is still a little dangerous nonetheless. However, when the canoe does hit something solid like the raft, nearly everyone in the canoe falls off their seat, which does look a little comical if you have ever seen that happen.

If a front steerer panics or sees that they might hit something, he can always ask the guests in his canoe to drag their paddles in the water. With both the front and rear RO's dragging their paddles hard in the water along with the guest's help, the canoes can come to a pretty quick stop if needed.

Flipping a Canoe Over

People sometimes ask if the canoes have ever flipped over. I'm sure this question is in response to the average guest having either experienced difficulty in maintaining balance in a canoe or has watched *America's Funniest Home Videos* where notoriously someone flips a canoe trying to get in or out. The fact is it is very difficult to flip one of the Davy Crockett Explorer Canoes. The reason is the canoes have air-filled ballast tanks making up the entire side of each canoe. These buoyant sides maintain the integrity of the balance point of each canoe. However, as was proven one of the years I was working, a canoe did indeed flip over. The circumstances, as I understood it from my friend Rob, who was actually working the very canoe that flipped over that day, was that the guests had been rocking the canoe quite a bit, allowing water to come in over the very low sides of the canoe. The middle of the canoe sits very low to the water with the gunwales of each canoe only about four inches above the waterline. While the canoes can't sink, because of the aforementioned ballast tanks, they can take on a lot of water but still remain above water, even when filled with guests.

However, when the amount of water in the canoe neutralized the ability of the ballast tanks to sustain balance, the group of rocking guests, who had been asked several times not to rock the canoe, leaned far enough that the center of gravity passed the balance point. It flipped completely over, dumping all the guests and the ride operators into the water.

Luckily, no one was hurt and the event occurred right by one of the piers that stuck out from the front side of Tom Sawyer Island, where all the guests, and the RO's could swim to safely. Because the water is only about four-feet deep at that point, most of the guests simply walked along the bottom of the river to the pier. Had the canoe flipped near the middle of the river, where the track is laid for the Mark Twain and Columbia, the depth of the river would have been about eight-feet deep. For this reason, the canoe RO's are instructed to maintain their path along the river as close to the shore as possible. However, there are several areas that the canoes must cross the middle of the river which the RO's must be wary of at all times.

Hooking and Other River Antics

Mischief on any of the attractions at Disneyland usually occurred when two things were present: Creative individuals working the attraction and limited supervision. In the case of the canoes, supervision was limited by the amount of territory we covered. It was simply impossible for a supervisor, one who oversaw many attractions, to observe the canoes every trip and everywhere along the river!

As a result of the limited oversight we had on the canoes, one thing that was occasionally done was 'hooking' another canoe. Hooking a canoe would cause the hooked canoe to turn completely around in the middle of the River. This was possible when the faster-moving canoe came up behind a slower one. The canoe coming up from behind angled the nose of his canoe so that it clipped the tail end of the canoe in front. Once the canoes met, the rear canoe made a hard turn, pushing the back of the canoe ahead of it around. There was nothing the slower canoe could do. The result was one canoe ending up facing sideways—or even pointing completely backwards—in the river.

The guests usually got a big kick out of the stunt, and the canoe that got turned around would have to have one side of the canoe paddle backwards while the other side paddled forward to help get the canoe turned back around and moving in the right direction.

Jaws

One year, a friend and I tried rather unsuccessfully to build a prominent shark's fin on a submerged platform that could be towed behind the canoe by a piece of fishing line. The idea was for the guests looking at the canoe from the Island or from the river walk around New Orleans Square to see a big shark's fin chasing the canoe. Unfortunately, or, from the perspective of potentially being fired: fortunately, we could never get the fin to work properly. We thought it would be a hilarious sight for people to see this big, black and gray shark fin swimming behind the canoe. With the movie *Jaws* still relatively fresh in the minds of everyone, since the original movie came out in 1975 with three sequels released in the ensuing years, we wanted to have some fun while at work.

This was just one example of how many of us working tried to come up with creative ideas to make other cast members or the guests laugh. Of course, Disneyland—or more specifically, supervision at Disneyland—tried to reign in many of these kinds of antics as they believed that it took away from the overall "Disneyland Show Element." (And, they are probably right!)

One of the other visual gags we would do would be to sit in the bottom of the canoe with just our head and arms barely above the rails. From a distance, it seriously looked like we had no lower body whatsoever, as the illusion looked like it was impossible to hide our body in the seemingly narrow space just below the waterline. (Magicians use this same optical illusion when they hide assistant bodies in what looks like impossibly small spaces.)

Splash Fight

On hot, summer days, occasionally kids and even adults would splash each other while on the canoes. While most people see the water as looking rather dirty and wouldn't consider getting soaked with that green wetness, others would ignore what the water looked like and proceed to scoop or splash paddles-full of water on to their friends in front or behind themselves. Actually, the river water was relatively clean. Disneyland had to color the water so the bottom of the river would not be visible and that the track for the two big ships, the *Mark Twain* and the *Columbia*, could not be seen. There were a couple of large pumps near *Big Thunder Railroad* that cycled the water and removed most of the leaves, sediments, and other litter from the water.

However, on one rather hot day, I was paired with a relatively new cast member named Grant. (Grant, years later, went on to become the keyboard player in a band I organized and subsequently moved on to other successful bands while continuing to work at Disneyland for over thirty years.) On this particular July afternoon, I was the front steerer and Grant was in the rear of our canoe when we had a group of guests on our canoe who insisted on splashing each other.

I stood up after the second round of splashing and asked the guests not to splash as there were people on board who probably didn't want to get wet.

"But we are all one family and we don't care if we get wet," the leader of the crew of sixteen guests explained.

The group was made up of mostly adults, a couple of teenagers, and a couple of senior adults. In my infinite wisdom, I had to ask, "You mean you ALL want to get wet?" I directed the question to the few older people in the canoe. They nodded their heads yes.

"We don't care," the older folks told me.

I glanced back at Grant who I think was slowly shaking his head, knowing I was a little bit on the crazy side of doing things. I smiled then took my five-and-a-half foot-long paddle with its large flat end and started shoveling water over everyone. The group squealed with delight and joined in the splashing. You literally could not see from one end of the canoe to the other through the spray of river-water. Luckily, we were just shy of the Indian Village on the back side of Tom Sawyer Island, where there weren't guests to witness the deluge. I was also hoping there were no supervisors hiding out in the back area as they occasionally did to check up on us that worked on the river. However, another canoe of guests did come around the bend. It was priceless to see the look of incredulity on their faces as they slowly passed us, witnessing the shower of river water that was engulfing our canoe.

After a couple moments of splashing fun, I acquired everyone's attention again and got them to stop. I informed them that we really had to keep paddling to get the canoe back to the dock, but they could splash each other in the process. By this time there was not a dry stitch of clothing on anyone, so it didn't matter if anyone got any more drenched. And, because it was such a hot day, the shower was refreshing. I also asked the guests that once we came back out to the area of the Park where others could see us to please not splash anymore as I could get fired. I'm sure, by this point, I could have been fired anyway! And, I'm sure Grant was thinking the very same thing.

Eventually we got the canoe back to the dock with the drenched guests, all laughing with delight at the unexpected dousing we gave each other. They each stepped out of the canoe that now had several inches of river water in the bottom.

Guests in line witnessing these soaking wet guests disembarking the canoe were gasping, wondering if we had gone under a waterfall or if the canoe had flipped over. They were probably wondering if they were about to get soaked as well. Some of them may have vacated the attraction at that point.

While Grant and I pumped the excess water out of the bottom of the canoe, with portable, battery powered pumps we kept on the dock, the grinning leader of the group of wet guests came back down from the exit and shook my hand.

"That was the best ride we have ever had here at Disneyland." He thrust a five-dollar bill into my hand.

"Oh, thank you. But, we can't accept any tips here in the Park," I explained, handing him back the five.

He reluctantly took the five dollar bill from me then suddenly thrust it into the pocket of my wet pants. "I'm not taking it back. You deserve it and you're keeping it," he said as he turned to join his family. It was the only tip I had ever received working at Disneyland!

For the past thirty years, Grant, my partner in the canoe that day, has alluded to the fact that I need to split the tip with him, as an ongoing joke. In reality, I'm sure at that moment in time, when I was shoveling water on top of sixteen guests Grant saw his short employment at Disneyland pass before his eyes. As a rookie, Grant thought for sure the event would cost me—and him—our jobs! Even to this day, we kid each other about that event which happened over thirty years ago! Grant is still gainfully employed by Disneyland, in fact, a manager of a portion of the Park!

Meeting Women

As mentioned earlier, the canoe ride operators were considered the "rock stars" of the Park for various reasons. In terms of the freedom we had, the physical workout we got, and the costumes themselves, the canoe guides seldom were short on dates. Most of the canoe guides became targets of many girls and young women's affection. (And even a number of more "mature" women, too, as several canoe RO's may or may not admit to!) Among the many romances that blossomed, (many lasting a day and others leading up to marriages!), there were many strange events dealing with women while working at the Park. For the most part, every day was considered an 'opportunity' to meet someone new. It was a lot like when we used to sneak into the Park as teens and meet girls on the dance floor or while walking through Disneyland. Working at the Park made the task of meeting women literally as easy as saying "hi."

Not Everyone Was Sane

One day, after meeting a young lady who worked in the Park, she greeted me near Harbor House where our time cards were kept and all cast members passed through. Not knowing anything about her, I was friendly and maintained a pleasant conversation with her as we walked out to our cars.

Nothing even remotely resembled an interest in her from me, other than a friendly casual conversation that lasted only the amount of time it took to walk to our cars in the cast member parking lot. The next day, a friend working in the Park told me about this girl who was talking all about her pending wedding to ME...that she was going to wed me on the Mark Twain, right there at Disneyland. I found out that it was the same girl I had walked out to the parking lot with the day before.

After tracking the girl down, I confronted her and in very specific terms, told her that I didn't even know her and that her telling others in the Park that we were getting married was unacceptable. Even while I made it very clear, I heard a few days later that she had again told someone else that she was going to marry me!

Obviously, this girl had some problems, certainly not only problems that were making me uncomfortable, but a delusional state of mind that couldn't be healthy when working at a place surrounded by tens of thousands of guests and hundreds of co-workers.

My next stop was to request supervision step in and advise the girl that she was not to have any contact with me nor discuss anything about me with anyone who worked in the Park. After that, I never saw the girl again. I have no idea if she quit, was fired, or was sent to spend time in therapy.

For the most part, everyone that I worked with, from my fellow Ride Operators to those in Merchandise, Foods, and in Janitorial joined in the prevailing spirit of working at a magical place where guests came to experience the magic for which we were all at least partly responsible. Every day, most of us came to work with a smile on our face; there was a tangible sense of anticipation. We knew we were going to make a lot of people happy, which in turn made our employment at Disneyland seem so much more than us just "doing our job".

While many old-timers became somewhat jaded and dismissed the sense of wonder and magic that the Park instilled in so many guests, most of us who were not so jaded and looked forward to coming to work with such feeling of anticipation that I think many of us would have worked at Disneyland for free.

The Dating Scene

As I've mentioned, gaining a date was as easy as showing up for work at Disneyland.

There were, of course, two sources for dates: fellow cast members and guests.

On canoes, it was not uncommon for RO's to see an attractive girl in line for the Canoe attraction. Judging where in line the girl was, and based on the number of canoes working the river that day, he could judge how many canoes he would have to pass to make sure he got that girl in his canoe. That was the hard part. The easy part was putting the girl into the boat, and whoever else was in the girl's party. Usually, whoever was going to be the front steerer unlatched the cue rope and led the guests to the canoe. Moving the desired 'date' either to the front or the rear of the canoe, depending on where the cast member was on the next trip was as easy as saying something like, "Let's have your group sit over here so we have a balanced canoe," or something to that effect!

Striking up a conversation, especially in the back of the canoe, was easy too. Asking where the young woman was from, if she was having fun at the Park, and what rides had she been on were the usual openers. In the back of the canoe, you were somewhat secluded from the other guests as it was very hard for guests to turn completely around while sitting on the narrow seats. With the exception of steering the canoe, the cast member in the back could carry on a very in-depth conversation with a guest sitting in front of them. If possible, the RO in the back would seat the girl in the single seat right in front of him. This made the potential discussion that much easier and intimate.

It was not uncommon to meet several women in one shift on canoes. If the RO wasn't busy that day after work, he would ask one girl if she would like to meet him at such-and-such time, at a prearranged location in the Park. Later in the day while still working, the same cast member, upon meeting another potential date would see if he could meet her in a location perhaps a little later than the first one.

It could be difficult if trying to direct a young lady to a specific location when she didn't know the Park very well. Most of the time, cast members would set up "dates" by telling them to meet them in front of *Sleeping Beauty's Castle*, on the draw bridge, since it was such a central and easily identified location.

Another place to meet was the entrance to what was then, *Mission to Mars* as there was an employee entrance right there and it was also adjacent to the cast member's locker rooms where most of us changed clothes before heading home.

What was usually very interesting was the response of many young ladies when they would see their cast member 'date', coming up to them in street clothes! Some might not initially even recognize the person until they call them by name or simply walk right up to them. Considering the girls we met had only seen the cast member in a Disneyland costume earlier, it was sometimes intriguing to see their reaction. It was almost like being on a blind date with only a previous picture as the hint. Yet, this intrigue usually heightened the girl's perception of what it might be like to be with the young man they had met earlier in the day.

As mentioned, sometimes a cast member might set up more than one date on the same day after work. Juggling dates, by setting them up an hour or so apart, allowed the cast member two things: One, if one of the girls didn't show up, he had a back-up date in the wings. Two, if his first date proved to be boring, uncommunicative, or not as appealing, he could excuse himself with an "I'm sorry. I've got to head home. I forgot I told a friend I'd meet him there," or some other fictitious excuse and subsequent apology.

While Disneyland was big, in such cases where a cast member might ditch one date and meet up with another, he ran the risk of running into the first date—while now with a new date! For most cast members, that risk was part of the territory and worth taking.

Blind Dates

Just like in school, some cast member dating involved leaving notes for a potential date. In the cast member timecard building, Harbor House, it was common to see dozens of hand-written notes left on timecards, notes to be found by the timecard-owner when he or she came into work the next day.

In my first year working in the Park, I became the recipient of one of these notes. However, my note was more like reading one of my *Hidden Mickey* novels! The cryptic clue read:

Dear Dave,
We love the way your wear your 'skins'. Love, your fan club.

Being fairly new, I pretty much blew off the note as a joke or a prank. I went into work with only a bit of curiosity of who may have written the note while working the first part of the afternoon. A little later that day, during my lunch break, my partner, Karl, was standing in line with me in the *DEC*, (the underground employee cafeteria below *Pirates of the Caribbean*), when he said, "I hear you've got yourself a fan club."

"What?" I asked. "How do you know about that, Karl? Did you see the note I got?"

Just then, Karl's girlfriend, Becky, came up to him and smiled at me saying, "Yeah, Dave. I understand you have a fan club!"

"Okay, you guys. What is this 'fan club' thing about?"

Becky said, "Well, without giving anything away, there are a couple girls who work in the French Market who want to meet you.

"Yeah, right."

"No, really! And one is right over there." Becky pointed to a group of girls all wearing the recognizable royal blue French Market dresses and white aprons.

I looked over at the three or four ladies and said, "Which one?"

Becky smiled. "I'm not saying."

"Thanks a million, Beck," I said with a little sarcastic tone to my comment.

"You're welcome, Dave," Becky sang back.

As it turned out, one of those girls in my so-called fan club was an extremely cute girl named Patty who met me after work that same day. We had a wonderful time going on some rides and getting to know each other. Her cousin, who had never been to Disneyland, happened to be in town. Together, Patty and I showed him all around the Park. All the while, Patty and I were feeling a strong attraction for each other, growing moment by moment. However, because of her cousin, we maintained our distance. Throughout the rest of the evening, it was a little like that first date I had with Sharon back when I graduated from intermediate school: We both felt that palpable sensation of knowing we liked each other. But, we both were trying to be respectful of her cousin that we didn't want to neglect in any way. We snuck little hand-holding moments in various lines and rides. Our hips would press together when in close proximity. But we held back from that first kiss; it was probably the most fun—but agonizing—time I had at Disneyland in all my years working there. Patty and I dated for much of the summer.

But, it didn't stick.

It wasn't uncommon for cast members to meet other cast members, either at work, at Disneyland-sponsored social or recreational events, or through other friends who worked at the Park. Imagine Disneyland being just like high school, only instead of people in the same classroom, you worked with them in themed areas. And considering the number of cast members in Merchandise, Foods, Operations, or even Security or Landscaping, in any given area, there were almost an unlimited number of people to meet and possibly date.

Security

Before my encounter with my 'fan club,' I had an even more *enlightening* experience with the opposite sex. I had been hired in early July of 1978 and my birthday was later that month just a few weeks after my being hired. That particular day I was working canoes and went on my normal break. We usually took our breaks with our canoe partner since a canoe team was relieved by a rotating pair of ride operators who gave each team their break.

As I walked with my partner that day towards the underground employee cafeteria below *Pirates of the Caribbean*, I was confronted by a female security guard. Only this wasn't one of the large male security guards. On the contrary, this Bear Country Security Guard was a tall, attractive woman who looked to be in her late twenties. I had seen her several times as I walked through the Park to and from the canoe dock as well as down in the employee cafeteria.

The woman stepped in front of me, making me stop dead in my tracks. Guests moving through the area had to suddenly flow around us like vapor trails following the contour of an airfoil. My eyes went to her chest; no, not for the obvious reasons. It was her nametag that was pinned to her vest, which was nearly at my eye level due to her being almost six inches taller than me. The nametag said her name was Jan.

"Happy Birthday, Dave," she said, standing directly front of me, effectively blocking any possible retreat.

"How did you know it was my birthday?" I asked. By now, my canoe partner had nodded to me the familiar guy-sign of "good luck" and "see you later".

"I have friends in administration," Jan said. She then changed her tone, "I have a present for you," she half-whispered. There was a glint of playfulness in her eyes.

"Really," I said, with a hint of disbelief. After all, I had only seen this woman a few times and probably only had said "Hi" to her even less. In reality, I had only been working in the Park for three weeks. Everything was so new to me that I didn't know what to believe or expect!

"I'd like to give it to you if you have time," Jan said with a most pleasant smile.

Both curious and skeptical, I said, "Um, sure. I'm game."

"Yes, you are," Jan whispered, raising her eyebrow. She turned and said, "Follow me."

Jan led me towards the exit of *Haunted Mansion*. I followed in her wake as she parted the sea of guests exiting the attraction as we moved against the flow. Off to the side of the exit of *Haunted Mansion* was an inconspicuous iron gate. Jan reached between the iron bars and pushed on a secret latch. With a click, the gate opened. She held the gate open for me and I passed through it, feeling the curious eyes of guests watching us go through this 'cast members only' gate. This was an area I was completely unfamiliar with. I followed the sway of Jan's velour skort as she then led me along a narrow concrete path that curved around the side corner of the *Haunted Mansion*. The walkway ended at a mysterious door, one that looked like it was the entrance to a crypt.

"In here," Jan said and held the door open for me.

I was beginning to feel like a short-lived character from a slasher movie being led to some unknown torcher chamber, never to be heard from again.

The door opened into a landing area for a steep flight of stairs. They led down into the underground portions of the Haunted Mansion.

"Ever been down here?" Jan asked as the door shut with a soft thud behind me.

"Never," I said, looking down the steep steps that obviously led somewhere under the *Haunted Mansion*.

"Well, follow me," Jan said as she moved down the steps. There were fluorescent lights that lit the stairway. As I descended further, I found that the stairs led to a narrow hallway that looked like it extended for at least fifty feet. The walls of the corridor were painted white and along both walls were an occasional door. I passed one of the doors where an engraved plate that was attached said, "Ballroom". Jan opened the door and we stepped into a darkened area that had a curtain covering whatever was beyond. After the door shut, Ian pulled back the curtain to reveal we were in the bottom floor of the 'ballroom' scene of the *Haunted Mansion*. Above us was the track which the guest rode their 'doombuggies' through the attraction. Before us were audio-animatronic figures dancing, each pair spinning on hidden tracks along the floor. To the left was an old organ with another audio-animatronic figure playing the ghostly theme song heard throughout the attraction.

I had read a book about Disneyland and knew that the organ had actually been a prop used in the 1954 movie, *20,000 Leagues Under the Sea*. The organ was indeed the same one that Captain Nemo, (played by actor James Mason), played onboard his submarine, "The Nautilus."

"Can we be seen by the guests?" I asked, actually thinking to myself, *Can I be fired for being down here?*

"No, we are away from the lights that illuminate the figures," Jan said, looking at the scene with as much awe as I was. "Hey, we can go onto the floor and dance!" Jan said pointing towards the dancing figures.

"I don't waltz surrounded by ghosts."

Jan laughed. "Okay. We better head back. I thought you might like to see down here. I really like exploring these areas."

"This is very cool," I said as we pushed back the curtains and then opened the door back in the stark, white corridor. "Thank you for taking me down here," I said, and then added. "Was that my present?"

Jan just smiled. "Head up the stairs," she directed me, following behind.

We headed back up the way we had come. As I reached the top step Jan reached out to my hand.

"Stand there," she said, referring to the top of the stairway landing. She moved up to the step one below mine, which, in essence, put her eyes level with mine since she was several inches taller than I.

"Happy birthday, Dave," Jan said in a conspiratorial voice. She put her arms around my shoulders and her lips on mine. The softness of her lips quickly subdued my surprise and I accepted her 'gift' with my own appreciation. My hands slipped around her waist and I was more than lost in her desire and affection.

I returned to the canoe dock with more than a little skip in my step. In fact, I was really starting to believe that Disneyland was indeed the "Happiest Place on Earth"... To work at!

Talented Cast Members

One thing about working at Disneyland is the generally high quality of people they hire. The level of imagination that went along with talent and a genuine sense of adventure among fellow cast members made working at Disneyland that much more enjoyable.

One of the things that encapsulated this was the publication of an 'underground' newsletter that was devised and secretly distributed throughout the Park's attractions, a newsletter that was called, "Jungle Drums...the Voice of the Jungle." As the title would infer, the five-to-seven-page newsletter was written mostly by guys working the *Jungle Cruise*.

The publication was in connection to an annual event known as the Banana Ball, which was one of the largest employee parties in all of Southern California.

Jungle Drums

The first publication I had ever seen of the Jungle Drums was in 1979. The issues summed up events such as Summer Softball and Canoe Races. It also highlighted events that usually occurred on the *Jungle Cruise*.

One such story was about a Jungle Cruise Guide named Chris who became so infatuated with a girl standing near the exit of the *Jungle Cruise* that he threatened to shoot himself with his Jungle Cruise blank-shooting Smith & Wesson. When the girl rebuked his attempt at a date, Chris put the gun to his head and pulled the trigger, thinking that he had taken all the blanks out of the pistol. Unfortunately for him, the gun indeed had one blank still loaded in the chamber. The gun fired and, although it was indeed a blank cartridge being fired, the explosive nature of the gunpowder shot out the barrel of the weapon and knocked Chris to the ground, with a bleeding gash near his temple. While he was not physically hurt as badly as his ego, Chris went to first aid and became the butt of many a joke thereafter.

The Jungle Drums newsletter poked fun at the Park, Supervision, the guests, and, as mentioned, fellow cast members. These were usually done in a literary version of the old *Rowan and Martin's Laugh In,* starting with a page of 'News Briefs' (presented, of course, by 'Fruit of the Loom'.) Examples of those stories included the following:

WED "Imagineers" announced today the discovery of a new substance which they hope to incorporate into the rock work at the Big Thunder Mountain Railroad attraction being built. Reportedly it is a combination of mashed potatoes from the Inn Between restaurant and refried beans from Casa de Fritos. A WED spokesman said the new space age material should be impervious to weather and will last hundreds of years.

And,

The growing concern over the duck population on the Rivers of America increased last Monday as several ducks dragged a small girl off the balcony of the Hungry Bear Lodge and fed her to its baby ducklings. A Park spokesman termed the incident, "Unfortunate but not serious."

And this,

In an inter-office communication this morning, Park culinary officials announced the introduction of a new dessert style item which will be featured Park-wide. The imaginative new "Frozen Water on a Stick" will be reasonably priced at 95 cents and also will be available to employees in the cast member restaurants.

In addition to funny and topical news briefs the <u>Jungle Drums</u> also featured several comical pages that started with, "You know you're a Lifer when..." or "You know you're Foreman material when..." followed by a list of funny—but often closer to the truth—descriptions of each. For example:

You Know You're A Lifer When...
　　　...your hair automatically stops growing just above the ear.
　　　...you wear your name tag in the shower.
　　　...your hat has left a permanent ring around your head.
　　　...every time you talk in public you put your hand up to your mouth. (Which you do when you spiel with a microphone on Jungle Cruise!)

Banana Ball

What started in 1969 as a *Jungle Cruise* end-of-summer party, held at various Elks and Ebell clubs and halls in Orange County, the Banana Ball became an Adventureland-Frontierland area party in 1974. Two years later, the Banana Ball became a Park-Wide affair held at the Orange County Fairgrounds.

Again, the creative juices among the Jungle Cruise ROs became legendary as this enormous party, attended by well over 1000 cast members, grew in both size and entertainment value. D.J.s, live bands, and all-you-could drink beer, for a single fee of $5, was truly a recipe for fun—if not disaster! However, at least in my years of working at the Park, I never saw an incident or heard of an incident of anything too outrageous. The worst we ever saw were a few cast members who came to work the next day at Disneyland with massive headaches!

In addition to the adventurous spirit such an 'end-of-summer' party as the Banana Ball would invoke, the Banana Ball featured some very funny special entertainment. The Banana Ball was like an adult version of a high school prom—minus the tuxes and formal dresses. Instead, cast members wore fanciful Hawaiian shirts, cute—if not in some cases very sexy—Hawaiian dresses, and, of course, the prerequisite plastic leis.

Mr. Bill Goes to Disneyland

At every Banana Ball the Jungle Cruise 'skippers' would show a movie they filmed in the Park. The first of these "Super-8" filmed movies included the documentation of guests in the Park who were dressed ridiculously or looked simply indescribable. Women wearing curlers in their hair, clothing that didn't match, extraordinarily obese people trying to fit on rides, all of which, of course, would be very frowned upon by today's politically correct censors!, and people doing nonsensical things in the Park.

However, with the popularity of the *Saturday Night Live* skit, "Mr. Bill," (a movie featuring an eight-inch tall doll made of Play Dough who would somehow always get mangled, flattened or disfigured in each episode), the Jungle Cruise operators filmed their version of Mr. Bill, called "Mr. Bill Goes to Disneyland."

A "Mr. Bill" Doll

The movie was hilarious, especially to all of us who worked the attractions or in the areas that Mr. Bill would experience his little "adventures" in. The movie started with Mr. Bill going to the Park with "Mr. Hands" driving Mr. Bill in a Volkswagen bug. Mr. Hands was the narrator who spoke with Mr. Bill but whom you would only see his hands gesturing. Mr. Bill first goes on the *Jungle Cruise*. For those unfamiliar with the attraction, the guests would enter the boats through two openings, stepping down onto one of the seats which the seat cushion had been removed. After all the passengers were on the boat, the cushion would then be replaced so the last guest could sit on the seat. However, in the movie, Mr. Bill is placed on the seat, BEFORE the cushion is replaced and Mr.

Hands says, "Mr. Bill, don't sit there, they haven't put the seat cushion down yet."

Then the cushion would be put on top of the clay doll and in the film a very large woman is seen sitting down upon the cushion. The camera pans back as the boat depart the dock with all the guests on board, and on the film you hear the famous, "OOOOHHH NOOOOO," that Mr. Bill would always say before getting flattened. In the next scene we see the boat return and the cushion is removed, revealing a completely flattened, pancake-like, Mr. Bill with his round mouth flattened around his round head.

The scenes in the movie included Mr. Bill falling off the *Skyway*, into the *Submarine Lagoon*, followed by a scene looking out one of the portholes in the sub and the view of Mr. Bill sinking slowly past in the water, gurgling his famous, "Oooohhh, nooooo!"

The final scene is Mr. Bill standing in the middle of *Main Street*, during the afternoon parade. We hear Mr. Hands say, "Mr. Bill, your standing in the middle of the parade," at which point we see a skipping costumed Alice in Wonderland coming up to Mr. Bill and suddenly soccer-kicking him down the street in full view of hundreds of guests. (Later, I found out that the cast member playing Alice that day got into a bit of trouble for her small part in the movie.)

Needless to say, the Banana Ball was always a hit and a great way to end the summer season. On top of the liberal amounts of 'refreshments', the number of beautiful girls wearing oftentimes very flirty tropical outfits, and the opportunity to dance and interact with everyone, created an atmosphere that was truly unique—if not creating a post-summer mystique that made most of us look forward to having one last fling!

As the end of summer approached, many college-aged cast members were getting ready to go back to college. Those who were teachers got ready to go back to their respective schools, and others were moving on to other jobs. Throughout the month of August, there was a growing feeling of anxiety experienced by most cast members. It was similar to how many felt when they were in their last year of high school: As the school year was ending, friends would be graduating and moving on, ending what was usually four years of friendships. At Disneyland, many of us knew that we wouldn't see some of our fellow workers again; others looked forward to the break and others still stayed on and worked during the fall and winter months.

It was undeniable: there a palpable feeling of deep friendships that had been cultivated through the course of working days and nights at Disneyland. Among some, there were love affairs that would blossom from those warm summer days and nights at the Magic Kingdom. There were those who met guests and maintained relationships—sometimes from long distances— and others who forged working relationships that would stand the test of time.

For every attraction, restaurant, and merchandise vendor, there were countless stories like those I've alluded to and others that I will expand upon in later chapters. But, for sure, each location inside Disneyland was truly a story waiting to be told.

Chapter 7

New Attractions... (Rides Too!)

Pirates

By my third year working at Disneyland, I was now considered a seasoned cast member, yet, I was still considered a Casual Employee that only worked during summer and holiday seasons. Still only working those seasonal periods, my status allowed me to anticipate returning to the Park with a sense of anticipation and eagerness. There was a fresh and exciting mystery of what the coming months held. Obviously, this sense of eagerness was more pronounced from my seasonal employment than if I had continued working in the Park throughout the year. I truly looked forward to coming back to Disneyland each summer, possibly in the same type of eagerness of when I returned to school each year after summer vacation. At school each year, there was the opportunity of seeing friends, wondering what teachers I would have and the like. At Disneyland, I not only looked forward to seeing many friends again, there was the anticipation of the unexpected that I think I was most drawn to. And yet, unlike school, I was also looking for that intangible "magic" that Disneyland offered—not only to the admission-paying guests, but also to those who worked in the Magic Kingdom.

Disneyland's Pirates of the Caribbean Entrance

There was also something about working Disneyland at Christmas that was appealing. I don't know if it was all the decorations in the Park or the Christmas spirit, or perhaps, it was because we had an opportunity to revisit our cast member friends for a couple weeks between summer seasons. Regardless, the coolness of December brought out the hot chocolate and the scarfs, and costume-matching jackets, and a feeling of joy and happiness that was unique to Disneyland during that holiday season.

I was in my final year of college at California State University, Fullerton; it was also known as "Cal State Disneyland" since so many cast members in college also attended the university a half dozen miles north of the Park in Fullerton. I had played tennis at CSUF, playing #1 and #2 singles by then I was now looking forward to coaching with my father at La Quinta High School in the Garden Grove Unified School District.

I was getting older.

My third summer, summer of 1980, I was invited to be trained on *Pirates of the Caribbean*. Working at Disneyland meant you could be trained on any one of the several attractions in your themed area of the Park. I had been hired into the area called *New Orleans/Bear Country* or NOBC for short, which meant I could be trained on *Pirates of the Caribbean, Haunted Mansion, Rafts, Keel Boats, Canoes,* or *Country Bear Jamboree.*

The *Pirates of the Caribbean* attraction, certainly a favorite ride among guests, was one of the more complex attractions in Disneyland. As one of the highest capacity rides in the Park, moving nearly 3500 guests per hour through the attraction, the ride-system featured as many as thirty boats moving through the ride at any one time. Two large water pumps maintained the water levels in both the upper load/unload area as well as the subterranean level where the majority of the show takes place, moving a total of 38,000 gallons of water per minute between the two ride level.

In reality, the Pirates of the Caribbean boats technically do not go underground, as is usually assumed since the boats with guests go down two waterfalls, dropping to a level nearly 30 feet below the load/unload dock. The ride flume actually carries the boats down to "street" level, the same level as the parking lot was at that time. (Later, part of this original parking area would become the Downtown Disney Resort area.) From Main Street, guests actually walk up a slight incline into the areas of Adventureland and New Orleans Square, and thus, the Pirates of the Caribbean waterfalls simply take boats down this grade into two large "ride-buildings" that house the majority of the Pirate's show. (There is also another ride-building to the west of Pirates for the Haunted Mansion attraction; in that ride, it is the "stretching room" elevator that takes guests down to this lower level. Today there is a newer ride-building to the east of the Pirates' building that houses the Indiana Jones attraction.) These buildings today are nicely "camouflaged" and well hidden now by the buildings on the north side of Downtown Disney. Before the major expansion of Downtown Disney and Disney's California Adventure (DCA), the areas of DCA and Downtown Disney made up the original parking lot for Disneyland. At that time, you could easily see the backs of the ride buildings for Pirates and Mansion as they were just beyond the tall Park fence and painted a pale pea-green.

In addition to the working components that move the guests through the show, *Pirates of the Caribbean* also has over 120 complex audio-animatronic figures, of which over 65 are realistic human figures that sing, dance, play instruments, and even imbibe on some "Disney brew"!

A note about the audio-animatronic pirates: Many of these human robotic figures were constructed to closely resemble the actual "Imagineers," (the Disney design team), who built them!

The computer room that controls all the sound, motion and lighting in the attraction is housed up a hidden stairway near the burning-city portion of the *Pirates of the Caribbean* attraction. It was always a shock to go in from the relative darkness of the Pirate's ride through a black door, and emerge in a stark white, high-tech, computer control room! In addition to the Pirates audio-animation computers and controls, this computer room also houses the computers that operate the Haunted Mansion show and audio-animatronic figures.

In the early years, Disneyland was going to use imitation skeletons on the *Pirates of the Caribbean* attraction. However, because the ability to create realistic skeletons was not available at that time, (the skeletons looked like cheap Halloween decorations!), Disneyland actually used REAL skeletons in the ride, skeletons they got from the medical center at the University of California at Los Angeles, (UCLA)!

Training on Pirates included two full days, where we learned each station for the attraction: Ticket-taker, at the front of the *Pirates of the Caribbean* building where the line of guests would first enter the attraction building, Load 1, also known as rear load as *Pirates of the Caribbean* usually included loading two boats simultaneously, Load 2—or front load. Then there was the unload station, on the opposite side of the ride-flume as the two loading stations, and finally, the Tower. The Tower was the control station for dispatching boats as well as keeping an eye on the twelve close-circuit television monitors that used infrared cameras to keep an eye on the boats moving through different areas of the ride...more on these monitors in a moment! In addition, we were trained on all the other parts of the attraction: from learning how to pull boats off the main ride flume and into boat storage to how to get guests out of the ride in case of an emergency. On busy days, we would have one additional station called Guest Control, where one Pirate's cast member would be stationed out in the queue area to help keep guests moving in the lines and making sure no one was taking cuts or trying to reconfigure of the line itself by changing the linked chains and connecting them to other posts.

Perhaps the most challenging stations were the load positions. There, you had to manage a large number of people: identify how many were in a group, break those groups up so that you could put four people in each row except for the last row, row five, which only held three people. You could get five "slender" guests in any of the first four rows but, it was a tight fit. Occasionally, you would have a group of five who INSIST they want to sit together. Well, we aimed to please, and fit them we sometimes did...even if they were carrying a little extra weight in the rear. Sitting cheek-to-cheek was a reality in those cases. However, we could not overload the boats since they sat fairly low in the water and the splashdown at the end of the two waterfalls with an overloaded boat would soak the people sitting along the rails.

After a few days of working the loading docks, getting the hang of directing people to 'rows' based on the number in each group became a piece of cake. However, if you were really tired and a few groups with a lot of people came in back-to-back, you sometimes had to reconfigure the rows so that each group could at least all ride in the same boat.

Unload was mostly made up of somewhat a mindless banter of: "Please keep your hands and arms inside the boat at all times; remain seated and please, no flash photography" prior to dispatching boats. After checking to see that everyone was safely seated, we would push a hidden button under the exit hand rails that turned on a lantern sitting on a stack of wooden crates on the corner of the dock, illuminating it green. This was Disneyland's way of keeping the theme of the attraction yet maintaining the technology and safety of dispatching boats in the right spacing. The green lantern was the signal for the cast member working the tower to safely dispatch the boats. However, the person in the tower could look out through the tower windows and see the boats from above. The Tower operator still had the ultimate responsibility to observe the boats and the guests before pushing the two black buttons on the dispatch board that launched the two loaded boats along the underwater conveyer belts, depositing them into the flume to start their pirate adventure.

Notoriously, just as the tower would dispatch the two boats from the loading dock, some guest would decide to stand up and try to switch seats, prompting an "E-Stop" (emergency stop) by the tower dispatcher who had a big, red button on the middle of the control panel that brought the boats to a dead stop. We usually kept a hand over the E-stop button until both boats from Load 1 and Load 2 had cleared the Tower.

Hit the Brake

As usual, cast members would sometimes figure out games to play on the guests for their own amusement or to entertain other cast members. These were attempts to have fun, usually at the guest's expense, but always in a fun way, not meant to really embarrass them.

One day, on the unload dock of Pirates, one cast member figured out a fun game to play called "Hit the Brake."

Because two boats would simultaneously be dispatched after being loaded with guests, two other boats, with guests who just finished their ride, would also move up to the loading dock behind the two boats that had just been dispatched. The first of these two boats coming up to unload, would move past the rear loading dock and move up to the front loading dock while the next boat behind it would move into the rear loading dock. Each boat would then, come to a halt so that those guests on board could exit to their right allowing the next passengers to board.

The game was played when the cast member on Unload would address the first row of the first boat as it began moving up into the loading dock area, asking the people in the front row of the boat very calmly, "Could you put your foot on the brake?"

Initially, the people in the front row looked up and noticed that they were coming up on the first loading dock. The cast member repeated the request with urgency in his or her tone. The guests, seeing they were passing the first loading dock—not realizing or remembering that there are TWO loading docks, suddenly believed they were heading out into the ride for another trip! Frantically, they started stomping on the floor of the boat trying to find the nonexistent brake they believed must be down there because they were not stopping.

Suddenly, the boat reached the front load and came to its normal stop. The cast member, with a straight face, yet looking very relieved said, "Oh, thank you. You found it."

By then the guests figured out that they'd had been had and that there was, of course, no brake on the boat floor and that the cast member had pulled their leg. It was sometimes hard to keep a straight face when watching guests stomping furiously before the boat came to a stop!

Finding Mickey

Grad Nites at Disneyland were always interesting. At 11pm, when the graduates arrived in the Park, Pirates was one of the busiest rides. However, by two or three in the morning, most of the kids would be in Tomorrowland dancing to the bands, or passed out on the benches throughout the Park from exhaustion or sleep deprivation. By two in the morning, *Pirates of the Caribbean*—and most of New Orleans Square—became a ghost town. On Pirates, we frequently dispatched boats with no one in them or with only a few people, or a single boy/girl couple, which we often termed "Love Boats".

With so few guests, we often had rotations in the ride that allowed for longer breaks for each cast member. And, because it was so slow, it was often hard to keep alert until closing at four in the morning when the Grad Nights ended. We had one particular ride foreman named Terry who hid an old, beat-up stuffed Mickey Mouse doll somewhere in the ride. He usually hid it when he first came on before the other Grad Night ride operators arrived. The game was for each cast member working on the ride, to try to locate the "Hidden Mickey," (hey, that would make a great title of a book!), during their fifteen to twenty-minute break. Understand that the ride is huge, taking up two immense buildings in which a maze of behind-the-scene areas is concealed by the ride façades similar to that of a movie set. Sometimes Terry hid Mickey backstage and other times the doll might be found onstage, actually in some section of Pirates. Cast members had to look for Mickey without being observed by the guests. One time Terry actually put Mickey on top of the talking skull, the one seen above the brick archway the boats go past, right before they head down the first waterfall. *Pirates of the Caribbean* ride at Disneyland offered two down-ramps or waterfalls that would plunge each boat into a wet 'splashdown'; the first waterfall is fifty-two feet long, the second shorter one was thirty-seven feet.)

The game was really a challenge; it was sort of a treasure hunt inside the ride for the cast members. Also, indirectly, the game forced the ride operators to review many of the backstage paths and secret entrances to the ride which became very important if the ride broke down. Anytime, if for whatever reason the ride did breakdown, we would have to escort the guests off the ride and walk them through the labyrinth of passageways to get them back into the Park. Usually, the main cause for a breakdown was when the ramp that brought the boats back up to the upper load/unload level broke down. If this happened, there was no way to get the guests back up to the unload dock and off the ride. In these cases, cast members would have to walk the guests out of the ride through these various emergency exits. Guests who actually went through one of these 101's, (the code number for a ride breakdown), generally loved it because they got to see some of the backstage areas of the Park! Sometimes secretly, guests would try and take pictures of areas they were seeing. All guests were told they were not allowed to take pictures of the backstage areas...but that didn't stop everyone.

The Mylar Table

Hidden deep in the bowels of the *Pirates of the Caribbean* attraction was an infamous table called the "Mylar Table." Located under the crisscrossing beams of scaffolding timbers supporting the façade of the ride sat a nine-foot-square table covered with carpet. It was on this table that maintenance workers laid out large sheets of Mylar plastic. They cut them into shapes depicting the fire scenes in the burning city on the Pirates attraction if they were worn or torn. The illusion of the various fire scenes was created using these Mylar sheets combined with orange lights and fans to flutter the plastic sheets to simulate flames.

Notoriously, some of the romantically involved couples who worked at Disneyland on the Pirate attraction somehow arranged to take breaks together. The Mylar table became the point of rendezvous for reasons I won't discuss here, but you can use your imagination. The Mylar table for decades has been the punch-line of many cast member jokes as well as the source of gossip for many who knew about its location—and reputation!

The "Mylar Table"

Smile! You're on Pirate Camera! (The 'Love Boat', Disneyland Style!)

One thing that many guests who are not real savvy about Disneyland don't know about is the fact that there are a dozen infrared video cameras on the *Pirates of the Caribbean* attraction.

These cameras are positioned to see, very clearly, several boats within each of the areas of the attraction. The feed from these cameras goes directly to the *Pirates of the Caribbean* Dispatch Tower. The dispatcher can observe people who are misbehaving, such as standing up in the ride, shooting flash pictures, or worse, trying to get out of the boats and damage or steal props in the ride.

In talking about Grad Nites, very early in the morning, when Pirates usually had more cast members working than guests coming on the ride), we inevitably would get a young couple to boat all by themselves. If the couple were from out of the area, or had not visited Disneyland very often, they usually didn't know about the cameras. Since the ride was one of the longest rides in the Park, there was a great deal of time for these couples to become, intimate while slowly drifting along the different scenes of the attraction.

One such night, the guy who was working the Tower called a couple of us working the load dock to come up the ladder to join him. Since the attraction was so slow, one of us at a time would climb the ladder up to the Dispatch Tower. There was only enough room really for two people inside.

There in black and white, since the close-circuit televisions only could display black and white images from the infrared cameras, one such couple thought they were indeed on the Love Boat. From one camera to the next, we observed this couple becoming quite adventurous!

After a few moments of black-and-white voyeurism, we each returned to our positions on the dock, to await the arrival of the 'love boat.' One of the cast members pulled some 3 x 5 inch index cards from the foreman's office located through a secret door in the side of the loading dock. With a thick black marker, he quickly jotted the numbers, 9.8, 9.6, 9.7 and 10.0 on the cards and handed them out to us working load/unload docks. Just as the 'love boat' pulled up to the unload position, four of us stood like

Olympic judges on the dock, then one by one posted the lover's 'scores' holding the cards in front of us.

Upon seeing the slightly confused look on their faces, I said, "You do know we have cameras on virtually every part of this ride, don't you?" Suddenly, the girl's face turned beet red. She took off toward the exit with her date trying to catch up with her.

On the wall in the foreman's office of Pirates of the Caribbean, someone once started a list called: Real Pirates... and everyone filled in their perceived completed sentence. Most of the sentences dealt with inside-jokes about the ride itself that were funny only if you worked the attraction. Some of the more creative lines included:

Real Pirates...
...like Guest Control for the ropes and chains. (Guest control was working the queue where the maze of chains directed guests.)
...think 19 in a boat is a light load. (15 was the typical fully-loaded pirate boat!)
...never push "E" stop. (Emergency stop button!)
...like 101's. (A 101 is a breakdown of the attraction.)
...know how to find the Mylar Table with their eyes closed. (See above!)

Not long after that list was exhausted, a new list was made: **Real Wenches...** some of those lines included:

Real Wenches...
...never pick up dirty diapers from the boats. (Self-explanatory!)
...heavily identify with the redhead. (The redhead is the voluptuous audio-animatronic female that was being auctioned off in the ride!)

...do their nails during a 101.
...love to spend their breaks on the Mylar Table.

Other lists came and went, like *"You know the summer is coming to an end when..."* and *"To make PPT, a casual employee should..."* (PPT stood for permanent part time which meant you worked weekends throughout the year...and a Casual Employee was everyone when they were first hired in to work at Disneyland...and those, like me, who only worked summers and holidays unless they applied for and were promoted to PPT.)

Becoming "Audio Animatronic"

Often, the way the rotations worked on Pirates, cast members could get a number of breaks during an eight-hour shift. With that many breaks, occasionally *Pirates of the Caribbean* cast members looked for things to do...ANYTHING to do! You could only spend so much time down in the PIT the cast member's cafeteria underneath *Pirates of the Caribbean*. (The PIT's real name is the DEC which stood for the Disneyland Employee Cafeteria. It got the nickname "PIT" not because of the quality of the food—which was really not bad—but, originally, the DEC had race cars painted on the interior walls, hence the moniker PIT, as in Pit Stop. It was, and ever since then—even as the walls no longer have anything resembling a car race—has been the cast member's nickname for the restaurant.

One idea we thought of doing was pretending to be an audio animatronic figure in the attraction itself. The best place to do this was in the jail scene near the end of the ride. This is where there are several jailed pirates trying to coerce a dog holding the key to the jail in its mouth with a bone and a rope! We would hop across one of the passing boats so we to move to the interior "island" portion of the ride, and walk behind the bars of the jail. Once positioned within the scene, mimicked the audio-animatronic figures, saying, "Here doggy, doggy...come on, boy..." while moving as if we too were mechanical. It was classic as guests in the passing boats would take pictures of the pirates in the jail, not knowing there were one or two 'real' pirates inside.

After a number of boats, we would stun the guests in a boat passing in front of us by standing up and looking at our watch, tap the real audio animatronic figure on the shoulder and say, "Hey Steve, Time to take your break."

Guest laughed or jumped with surprise at seeing a LIVE pirate, now wondering if any of the others in the attraction were also real.

On Pirates. (The "Pirate" on the far right is HUMAN!)

Funny—and Strange—Stories

Working at Disneyland was full of funny stories, strange events, and things that would pop up unexpected. It was also apparent that humans can be extremely, shall we say, 'brain-dead' or at best, at a loss for common sense? And then there were those who probably never had an IQ higher than my pet guinea pigs.

Let the Stories Begin!

My friend Jim told me his story of working *Haunted Mansion* one Grad Nite. As mentioned, Grad Nites were notorious for hormone-infused teenagers making the most out of any opportunity to get a little 'romance' in.

One night, Jim was working the Utility rotation on the *Haunted Mansion*. (Utility was walking through the ride in specific parts to check on guests in the clamshell "doombuggies" which were the ride vehicles for *Haunted Mansion*.) It was common to catch guests smoking, (cigarettes and 'other' smokables!), taking flash pictures, and even trying to get out of the moving vehicles to 'explore' the ride. On this particular night, or early morning, as the case may have been on a Grad Nite, a young man and his date were enjoying the relative privacy of their doombuggy and paying very little attention to the ride itself. During Grad Nites, the females had to wear either dresses or pantsuits to maintain the formality of the event. (Disneyland officials, early on, found that kids, when dressed up, tended to act more mature. Hence, this policy helped reduce many potential problems.) In this case, the young woman was wearing a dress that, as Jim discovered, seemed to have slipped down to her waist. Jim, while walking along the moving vehicles, saw the 'activity' that was taking place. Stealthily, from behind the couple, Jim snagged part of the hem of this girl's dress on a hook that extended out from under the ride vehicle. As the ride came to its conclusion, the girl, not surprisingly, was unable to get her dress off the hook. At this point, the ride operator on the exit portion of the ride had to stop the entire attraction so they could unhook this very embarrassed young lady's dress from underneath the vehicle.

The attraction hosts on both load and unload have what looks like a garage door opener on the belt of their costumes. This device is the button that they can push whenever it looks like someone needs assistance in getting on or getting off the attraction, or, as in this case, helping a very red-faced young lady who was trying to get her dress back on!

The IQ of a Brick

One afternoon, I was walking back to the locker rooms after a shift of working *Keel Boats*. As I passed by the entrance to *Pirates of the Caribbean*, I heard an incredible shouting match going on between two men. There were profanities being uttered every other word. It certainly was not what we considered appropriate behavior inside Disneyland.

As I approached the two men, I saw there was also a woman with them. By the ragged way the three were dressed, I felt like I was coming upon three homeless people arguing over a cardboard box. From the level of articulation—or lack thereof—that these people didn't make it to graduate school.

I tried to calm down the two men who didn't appear to be looking for a fight, just yet. Silly me, I had to ask what they were arguing about.

"I gave these two a ride to Disneyland because they said she would have sex with me if I did," the first man explained rather loudly. I was sorry I asked.

"No, I never said I would have sex with you, I said I would sleep with you." She was missing one of her front teeth. This was more than an issue of semantics.

"Liar," the first man replied.

"She ain't no liar," the other man piped in defending her.

"You both are," the other man pointed out, using some additional swear words to drive home his point.

This was going to require security personnel and needed to be handled away from all the guests who had gathered around to see how this was going to end up.

I immediately used my walkie-talkie and placed a call into security. It wasn't more than five minutes that I had a pair of very imposing security guards at my side. The two guards escorted the threesome to the security office to figure out just who owed who what.

I never did find out what the outcome of that exchange was.

One Strong Marine

Working around dusk on Pirates, we heard a lot of commotion near the area of the *Jungle Cruise* and the *Swiss Family Tree House*, which would become the Tarzan Tree House years later. At that time, there was no Indiana Jones attraction between the Tree House and the Jungle Cruise River.

The *Swiss Family Tree House* was a walk-through attraction where the large man-made tree supported a recreation of one used in the Disney movie, *Swiss Family Robinson*, a movie made back in 1960.

A very strong man was having a disagreement with his girlfriend while the two meandered up the steps of the tree-house attraction.

Suddenly, he pushed his girl to the side and picked up a bench that was bolted to the wood planks of a platform high up in the tree. In a fit of rage, the man tore the bench from its base moorings, and threw it overhead through the tree branches into the Jungle Cruise River. It narrowly missed a passing Jungle Cruise boat full of guests.

Luckily, the attraction's hostess got on her phone and called security. Quickly, security appeared and ushered the man—who was either intoxicated or strung out on some drug—down to security. He was then arrested by Anaheim Police for public intoxication, disorderly conduct, and destruction of private property.

I was just glad it was the bench and not his girlfriend that ended up in the Jungle Cruise River!

The Transition Tunnel

On Pirates, there was a section of the boat ride that moves the guests from the last scene in Ride Building One, the treasure room scene, into the first scene in Ride Building Two, the pirate ship firing cannons at the fort across an expanse of water. There is a short, dark tunnel between these two scenes that is called the "Transition Tunnel." Today, there is a projected image of Davy Jones from the *Pirates of the Caribbean* motion picture on a film of mist in the transition tunnel.

On breaks, occasionally, cast members went down to the tunnel through a secret entrance near the PIT cast member cafeteria. We often would simply stand very still very close to the ride flume in the darkness of the tunnel. Eventually, a guest would spot us, at which point, we would move or take a step. The sudden movement of a person in the dim light of the tunnel always startled guests.

Pirate's was a huge ride with so many elements that is was hard to be bored working the attraction. There was a powerful sense of control when working the Tower, dispatching the boats from the loading dock, checking the cameras on the ride, and the ability to project your voice through speakers within specific portions of the ride. Telling people to sit down, to quit taking flash pictures, or cautioning them about anything else guests were doing that was not acceptable, always made ROs feel in charge. But, while Pirates offered many interesting and fun adventures, it was not my favorite attraction to work.

The following summer, I was trained on a new ride!

Chapter 8

Keel Boats: Same River, Bigger Boat

By year four of my working at Disneyland, supervision discovered I had a personality that was applicable for spieling and interacting with guests, delivering part of the show. I enjoyed the opportunity to talk to guests, tell jokes, and handle large groups of people. From my years of working canoes, I had a good understanding of how to steer river craft safely and I knew the River as well as anyone. In fact, I was now the steerer for my own *Bad News Canoes*, our cast member men's canoe team. We were one of the top three teams each year for my final four years in the Park.

Thus, I 'got the call' from supervision who selected me to be trained on the *Mike Fink Keel Boats*, a ride that was part *Jungle Cruise*, part *Davy Crockett Explorer Canoe*, and part *Mark Twain*. I also had the opportunity to be part comedian!

The Bertha Mae, one of two Keel Boats operating at Disneyland. Note the double-deck seating and the long keel used to steer the boat.

Moving from one of the highest capacity rides in the Park, Pirates, to the Keel Boats, the lowest capacity ride in the Park, I went through a bit of culture shock. The entire Keel Boat fleet was made up two boats, the *Bertha Mae* and the *Gullywhumper*. Each boat carried about forty passengers. The boats were designed with an upper, open-air deck that sat twenty people, and a lower interior cabin that could fit six people in three separate cabin areas, each with large openings for the passengers enter and exit as well as to see out.

Like our Adventureland counterpart, the *Jungle Cruise*, the Keel Boats involved piloting a motorized boat and pointing out the sights along the way, adding humor everywhere possible. However, unlike the *Jungle Cruise* attraction where the skippers had a lot of things along their river to point out and a number of prepared jokes to choose from, the Keel Boats only had the same River around Tom Sawyer Island that the canoes, the *Mark Twain*, and the *Columbia Sailing Ship* circumnavigated. Those rides had very little spiel about the things along the river. The items around

Tom Sawyer Island—and the Island itself—didn't lend themselves to a lot of jokes as many of the scenes on *Jungle Cruise* offered.

Keel Boat History

Based on the Walt Disney television shows, and movies, *Davy Crockett's 169 Boat Race* and *Davy Crockett and the River Pirates*, the *Mike Fink Keel Boats* were small, free-floating, double-deck boats.

Because the boats were fairly top heavy when fully loaded, this design issue was most likely the cause of the closure of the ride in 1997:

On May 17th, 1997, a fully loaded, <u>Gullywhumper</u>, one of the two Keel Boats at Disneyland, began to rock back and forth. The cause for the rocking was a group of guests who had come to the park together and thought it might be fun to lean side to side to see how far the boat could list. At some point, the center of gravity was pushed too far and the boat literally capsized in the Rivers of America, dumping the fully loaded boat of passengers into the River. Neither boat was returned to service. In fact, the <u>Bertha Mae</u> was sold on a Disney eBay Auction for $15,000. It was labeled, "Unseaworthy."

The *Gullywhumper* was returned to Disneyland, remodeled to resemble the actual Keel Boats, those used in the 1800's, and the style of Keel Boats that were depicted in the Disney movies and television show. It now sits as a prop, anchored—actually looking like it is half-sunk—just before the settler's cabin on the right-hand side of the river after you pass the canoe dock.

Keel Boat Operations

On the Keel Boats, we did have an SOP Spiel, Standard Operating Procedure, which was about as dry—and quite frankly, as insipid—as any spiel could be. The SOP Spiel for the Keel Boats probably hadn't been updated since the ride debuted six months after Disneyland opened in 1955. One of the main reasons the Keel Boats existed was that they were the only river craft capable of towing the *Mark Twain* or the *Columbia* back into their docks if either big boat became stranded in the river. Luckily, the Keel Boats did offer the opportunity for a lot of improvisational dialogue for each driver.

One of the unique things about the Keel Boats was the fact that they were the only motorized craft not on a track and they traversed all the way around the Island. The *Tom Sawyer Island Rafts* were not on a track either, however, they only moved the short fifty-foot distance between their raft dock on the Island and the raft dock on the mainland in front of New Orleans Square.

On the Keel Boats, we had the freedom to drive nearly anywhere along the river. That even included doing 'donuts' in the middle of the river on the back side of Tom Sawyer Island when there weren't any other canoes or boats around. Donuts were just like doing donuts in a car: Turning as tight of a turn as the steering linkage would allow, and gunning the throttle, you could form a circle in the river with the boat leaving a donut-shaped backwash from the propeller.

And unlike the *Jungle Cruise*, we actually had to spiel *and* steer our boats. (*Jungle Cruise* boats are on a track.) To steer the Keel Boat, you used a long keel that curved down from the back of the boat and connected to the rudder. There was a throttle on a control console in front of us used to go forward or backward. And we also had to hold a microphone in order to spiel. Now, most of us were born with two arms and two hands. What I just described would require three hands: One to steer, one to throttle up and down, and one to hold the microphone. Add the fact that when I was first working the ride, we also had a spot light we used to point out things along the river when we operated the boats at dusk. Now we needed four hands!

We usually simply steered with our hip, throttled with our left foot, and spieled holding the microphone in one hand while with the other, we pointed out sights along the river with our spot light. Being able to perform all of those tasks—without running into things—required practice!

And, considering we couldn't even see out the front of the boat because the superstructure of the boat completely blocked our view, we also had to peer around the bulk of the boat to see if anything was in front of us. It always reminded me of the way Charles Lindbergh had to fly his *Spirit of St. Louis* airplane in 1927 in crossing the Atlantic Ocean. We had to use the curves in the river to see if canoes were nearby. Since the canoes were so low and the Keel Boats sat high up in the water, it made it even more difficult to see the canoes if we didn't spot them earlier. If you are thinking this story includes crashing into a canoe, I must apologize. At least during my tenure working the Keel Boats for two full summers, not one Keel Boat ran over a canoe.

However, I did have one slight crash: In coming around the turn in front of the Barrel Bridge on Tom Sawyer Island, my steering linkage broke and I could only turn the boat the slightest bit. Discovering the broken rudder while going full speed, I tried to lean hard on the Keel but got no response. Throwing the throttle into full reverse began to slow me down. However, I could tell I still had enough speed that I was going to hit the Island just west of the Barrel Bridge. I told everyone on the boat, "Hold On!" Luckily, the Island is surrounded by tall reeds that grow naturally near the water's edge. We rammed into the Island. The reeds cushioned the blow and no one fell off their seat. I found I could turn to the right but only fractionally to the left. Through a little maneuvering, I was able to reverse and then slowly steer to clear the Island. Luckily, there were only two right turns around the last part of the Island, which made it possible to make it back to the dock.

Keel Boat Spiels

With only three operators working the Keel Boats when one boat was running, four guys if both boats were running, we had a tight-knit core of ROs working the ride. Only males worked the Keel Boats at that time, and we created our own rotation. With one boat on, one guy would be on the dock taking tickets, one guy on the boat, and one guy on a break. With two boats, we added one additional ride operator on the second boat, which shortened our number of breaks considerably. However, with one boat on, each of us had a twenty-minute break every hour along with a half-hour lunch. We had so many breaks with one boat on that we actually got more bored being *on* a break than working the attraction!

Because we were not structured to follow a specific SOP spiel, even supervision said to NOT use the SOP spiel, we improvised and shared jokes, and even made some jokes up on our own.

One of my contributions to the ride was changing the opening spiel. Originally it went like this:

"Howdy, Hi all you pioneers and buccaneers, in-laws and outlaws, city slickers and finger lickers and everyone else...welcome aboard the Mike Fink Keel Boats..."

One day working on the dock, I started writing down all the words that ended in "eer." I then used that list to create the more creative, and certainly more difficult opening spiel that became the staple spiel for years by numerous ride operators on the Keel Boats:

"Howdy, howdy, hi to all you pioneers, buccaneers, engineers, souvenirs, chandeliers, cashiers, boutonnieres, frontiers, racketeers, brigadiers, mountaineers and musketeers, and all you in-laws, outlaws, grandmas, grandpas, Cole slaws, attorneys-at-law, big ones, little ones, Injun fighters, wild horse riders, city slickers, finger lickers, cow poke, city folk, sod busters and feather dusters, and all you lovely, lovely ladies…and all you other ladies too, welcome aboard the Mike Fink Keel Boats."

Our spiels would point out the canoe dock:

"Look at all those people waiting to paddle their brains out!" And then as we passed the Hungry Bear Restaurant: "Now there on the left is the Hungry Bear Restaurant where you can get a world famous Bear Burger. Of course, you can always tell the people just get'n done eat'n…they're the ones hang'n over the rail'n!"

Some of you who are a bit older may remember the original burning settler's cabin with the dead settler laying on the slope in front of the burning cabin with an arrow through his chest, which in more recent times became a more politically correct cabin without the dead settler and no longer burning, instead a nice garden growing out in front of the log cabin. With the original scene our spiel would be something like this:

"Does anyone hear smoke?" Wait for everyone to hear the cracking sound of the burning cabin. "Oh, my, there's ol' uncle Jed, lay'n out in front of his new cabin…looks like the local Injun's threw uncle Jed a 'house

warm'n' party. Oh, and it looks like Jed got all dressed up for the 'casion...he put on his new 'Arrow' shirt!"

Approaching the Indian Village on the left side of the river, a few jokes were passed around by Keel Boat captains. One that dates back to the original SOP was:

"That thar is the Pinewood Indian Village...called the Pinewood Indian Village because...well, that's what they're all made of...Pine Wood."

But the most creative and, in my opinion, the funniest joke was a longer-winded one, usually told when you had a little time to kill before moving on around the river:

"That Injun Village is very famous, actually making it into the Guinness Book of World records: Seems the chief back there in the back, the guy with the fancy feather headdress on, wanted to use the little chief's teepee...the teepee to go pee pee one night. Since it was so dark out, the chief asked one of his friends, an electrician, to put in a light bulb inside the pee pee teepee so he could see see when he went pee pee. Afterwards, the chief was surprised to learn that it was the first time in the history of man that anyone had ever wired a head for a reservation."

On the right side of the river were the Injun Burial Grounds...

"Where just the other day, I saw them bury a V-8."

There were many other jokes that other operators had come up with over the years. Some of the most fun we had was talking to the guests while we waited for the Mark Twain or the Columbia to move down the river a ways. Since the two big boats were the slowest craft on the river, we would end up getting stuck behind the big ships if we took off right behind them.

Asking guests,

"Where're ya from?"

"Kansas."

"Sorry?"

"Kansas!"

"Yeah, I heard you the first time. I said I was sorry!"

Or,

"Where're ya from?"

"Washington."

"Washington? Is that Washington AC or DC?"

Confusion would be on their faces. **"AC—Above California?"**

"Oh, yes!"

Or, finally,

"Where're ya from?"

"Nebraska"

"Well, welcome to civilization!"

Most Fun Keel Boat Game

As far as I know, no one else had ever played my favorite game while driving the Keel Boats, in fact, I don't know of anyone who even *knew* about this little trick!

After the Indian Village and the Injun Burial Grounds, the next curve in the river was a left turn. At this curve, on the right side of the river and up ahead of the boat there were a few large rocks that sat right on the edge of the Island in a clearing between the reeds that grew around the Island. Inevitably, guests loved to take a break from walking around the Island and sit on these rocks. Sometimes they would put their feet in the water or just rested with their feet on an adjacent rock. One day, I noticed that if you took the curve to the left in the boat fast, it would create a wave in the river. I saw that the water first would slowly recede from the edge of the shore of the Island before developing into a full wave that came back towards the rocks. The shape of the rocks and the curve of the river at that point made for the perfect funnel that would cause the incoming wave to crash between the rocks forming almost a geyser—right where people were sitting!

If I made the turn coming up to this left hand turn and saw there were people sitting on the rocks, I gunned the Keel Boat engine, made the hard left hand turn, and threw the throttle into full reverse so my Keel Boat would suddenly stop in the middle of the river. I would instruct all my passengers on the Keel Boat to wave to the people sitting on the rocks at the edge of the river, telling them that indeed a huge wave would form and splash the people sitting there. The idea of being in on a conspiracy was inviting to everyone. They all started waving, yelling "hi" to the people sitting on the rocks.

All the riders on my boat could see the water recede and then the wave start to form. The unsuspecting guests sitting on the rocks were too busy waving to the people on my boat to notice. I would whisper on my microphone to my guests, "Okay, keep waving, here it comes..." and suddenly the wave my Keel Boat made crashed onto the rocks shooting water up between them, soaking the people sitting there.

It was comical, if not a little bit of an underhanded way to get some laughs on my boat. Most of the time, the guests on the Island laughed it off after jumping up from the rocks in haste to unsuccessfully avoid getting wet. I heard the laughter all through the boat and even after the ride was over, people giggling over the event.

Finding Death

Indirectly, the Keel Boats will always remind me of death at Disneyland. While there have been a handful of deaths in the Park, I was directly involved with the discovery of one guest who had died.

It was two in the morning, the summer of 1983, June 4th, when during one of the many Grad Nites hosted at the Park, two teenaged boys decided to commandeer a maintenance rubber boat, a skiff called a "Zodiac". The small boat was chained up in an area that was off-limits to guests. The boys entered the area and found the skiff was only tied up to the dock, not locked up. It was being used by technicians to take sound equipment to the River Stage for the scheduled show. The boys were able to start the motor on the back of the rubber raft and took off towards the back side of the Island.

That early in the morning, it is very dark, especially around the rear side of Tom Sawyer Island. There are no lights to speak of. One of the Park security guards saw the boys just as they took off in the skiff and immediately called supervision and the security office. Several supervisors boarded a Tom Sawyer Raft and took it to the back side of the Island, knowing the boys would not be able to go all the way around the Island because they would be fully exposed the moment they came around toward Frontierland.

Unexpectedly, the supervisors came upon the skiff crashed against the first rock of the Keel Boat Rapids. When the supervisors arrived, the nose of the skiff, deflated from the impact with the rock, had one of the boys was still on the boat.

The boy said that his friend must have gotten scared and swam over to the Island or across the river to keep from getting caught.

I was working that night not as a ride operator but as Guest Control for the River Stage show. I got a call from my foreman to meet some supervisors on the Keel Boat Dock. Since the Keel Boats had a powerful spot light, and I was the only Keel Boat Driver working in the Park at the time, since the Keel Boats were closed at night, I jogged over and unlocked the Keel Boat. I started the motor to join in the search for this wayward teen that was thought to probably be hiding out along the bank of the river.

We had perhaps a dozen security guards combing the mainland side of the River. The heavily foliaged area was an uninhabited area that ran between the Hungry Bear Restaurant and the Pinewood Indian Village.

A number of other security guards were also looking in the trees on the back side of Tom Sawyer Island, near where the Zodiac skiff had encountered the rock in the river. I was cruising back and forth along that stretch of the river shining my spot light in and all around the trees and wild brush that grew on both sides of the river, helping the guards who were combing that area.

Suddenly, on my walkie-talkie, I got a call from my supervisor, Ralph. He asked me to turn around and come back over to where the Zodiac had hit the rock. The skiff had since been pulled out of the water and onto another raft that had come over to the scene. I brought my Keel Boat right up near the spot of the impact where Ralph was on the corner of the raft that had been driven right up toward the same spot.

"Shine your light down here," Ralph asked.

I pointed the powerful beam into the water where Ralph was leaning over the edge of the raft. I remember watching reach into the water. What looked like a brown paper bag lying about a foot under water was, instead, the back of the jacket the second boy who had been in the skiff was wearing. When Ralph pulled the jacket up, he also pulled up the boy still wearing the jacket out of the water. Two security guards helped pull the boy onto the bank of the Island.

Knowing that we had been looking for the kid for at least twenty minutes or so, it was a given that the boy had died. He drowned in less than four feet of water.

I'll never forget the image of my light being shown onto this pale, purple-faced boy, wearing a suit, tie, and sport coat. I'll also never forget the next words I remember hearing from my walkie-talkie, a command from the head of security now standing over the dead boy: "Call the coroner's office and get a Polaroid down here right now."

The next day, I was further saddened to learn the boy had just turned eighteen the day before he died. He and his friend had been drinking alcohol prior to their adventure. The boy was from New Mexico. All I could think about were the images that were implanted in my mind from the morning before. Also, I was imagining who, from Disneyland, was going to be the unlucky person who would have to call the parents to inform them of the tragedy.

Keel Boat Rapids

Cultural Differences

Working Keel Boats one afternoon, I stood on the dock in front of a large crate that was our impromptu work station. Facing out over the River, I watched for the next Keel Boat coming in and generally, enjoyed watching the traffic on the River. There was a section of the dock to my right that was open, where exiting guests left a boat, while the next group of passengers waited behind a sectioned-off area of the dock, separated by a rope that could be removed to let the new passengers get on board.

While I was recording the hourly count numbers on a clipboard, I glanced down and saw a stream of liquid running down the dock. I turned, shocked to see a seven or eight-year-old boy urinating on the dock. He had ducked under the rope and was standing up near the planter behind me. I was taken aback and asked the kid, "What the heck are you doing?"

"No English," the boy said quickly zipping up his pants and scampering back under the rope, obviously knowing what he had been doing was not acceptable. The boy moved behind a large Hispanic woman who I told quietly, "there are bathroom just up the walkway."

"No English," the woman, obviously the boy's mother, said.

I just shook my head and turned to put "Barf Dust," wood shavings that absorbed throw up. Now I had to use them to absorb urine. I sprinkled them over the trail of yellow liquid, some running off my dock and into the River.

In a moment, the next Keel Boat came into the dock and after I tied the front mooring line to the dock post, I walked over to Paul who had been piloting the boat and told him discreetly what had just occurred on the dock and why there was barf dust in a trail leading toward the River.

Suddenly, in remarkably good English, the Hispanic woman started yelling at me, "I know what you are talking about. You are talking about my son!"

I turned and looked at her, tilted my head, and said, "No English?"

She clammed up after that. I realized that there was a vast difference between cultures. Things that we considered completely unacceptable to me were not even thought about by others.

Taking a Dive

When a Keel Boat came into the dock, the operator working on the dock would use a long wooden pole with a metal hook on the end to grab the thick, braided mooring rope on the front cleat of the Keel Boat. He tossed the rope onto a heavy round pylon at the side of the dock. This was often done in a single, flipping move that was as athletic as it was artistic, especially when the rope landed around the pylon on the first try. This rope held the front end of the Keel Boat against the dock and when the boat was loading and unloading guests.

When the boat was loaded and ready to take off, the pilot reversed the engine backing the boat up, taking the slack off the front mooring rope. The dock operator removed the end of the rope from the pylon, tossed it back onto the bow of the boat, and then use the long wooden pole to push the front end of the Keel Boat out toward the middle of the River. This was because the Keel Boat Dock was right up against what was called "Fowler's Harbor", the larger dock used to store the large sailing ship, "Columbia" when she wasn't being used or the Mark Twain if it was being worked on; Fowler's Harbor had rear doors like a canal lock, which when closed, permitted maintenance to pump the water out of the dock and turn it into a dry-dock to work on the hull of either big boat.

One of the funny things we did was when we were pushing the Keel Boat out toward the middle of the River we leaned way out over the water while holding onto the end of the wooden pole. It always looked like the operator was going to fall in, considering how far we could lean out over the water, before pushing on the end of the pole to get back upright on the dock.

When the dock worker pushed back upright onto the dock, the boat pilot mentioned to his boatload of guests, "Let's give 'Lighting' a big round of applause." The operator who had leaned out over the water would take off his hat and hold it out as if the guests were going to throw him money as a tip. Ironically, people often actually tossed money across to the guy who would usually catch the coins in his hat. The guests waiting in line would see this and kids and adults would get coins ready for when it was their turn to be on the boat so they could toss them next.

We got so that we put all the coins in a tennis ball can that we hid in one of the dock-boxes on the Keel Boat dock. Each summer, the money we raised from these tips was used to buy refreshments for my mid-summer party, which I usually threw at my house!

One time, a woman was taking my picture and said, "Hold it" right when I was fully stretched out leaning over the water. Instinctively, I tried to hold the position a moment longer since she was trying to take my picture. The moment was a moment too long. I didn't have enough length of pole left to push back. I went into the water! The woman was kind enough to send the picture of me both leaning—and falling—into the River!

That was the only time I had ever been in the River unintentionally. After both years of winning the canoe races, our teams would always jump in the water! Generally speaking, I preferred making my own decision about getting wet.

Leaving the Park

It was the summer of 1983 when I gave my two-week notice that I was quitting the Park. I had been teaching high school and coaching tennis at my alma mater, Garden Grove High School. I needed to give up working summers and holidays at Disneyland so I could concentrate on teaching and coaching. I arranged so that my last day working would be the day after the finals of the Canoe Races.

Celebration of our victory!

The canoe races, for the cast members at Disneyland, were always one of the highlights for me working at the Park. As a competitive tennis player and coach, I relished the competition that the canoe races provided. It was truly a team effort all the way through each race.

In the previous two summers, my men's team, after upsetting Engulf and Devour in 1980, finished respectively, 2nd and 3rd. I really wanted to go out victorious in my final summer and symbolically leaving the Park as a Champion. I put together a great team that year, one that resembled the make-up of my team that won in 1980.

Like that first year, we went into the finals with the fastest time. But this year, we were considered the favorite.

Making this final even more meaningful was that it was the first time my parents and sister came out to watch the races. Knowing they were there, I was very anxious about the races, putting perhaps more pressure on me. As it turned out, my father passed away the following year; in hindsight, it was very special to have him there watching me lead my canoe team in something that was as exciting as it was competitive!

As the fastest team going into the final, we were the last team to race.

All eyes were on us as the starting gun sounded. We had a solid start with everyone paddling in good rhythm and cadence. As we came around the final bend, everyone on my team dug in with an explosive kick to the finish line. Everyone in the viewing areas was screaming as the large digital clock stopped as we crossed the line.

This time, we didn't need to see the tenths of a second to see if we had won. We ended up winning by three seconds...which may not seem like much considering that each canoe team must paddle the five-eighths of a mile journey around Tom Sawyer Island and anything can happen. However, typically, less than three seconds separated first place from fourth place in previous years.

I still remember our first victory: the year we won by a mere four tenths of a second. The year we finished second, we lost by only two tenths of a second! And the year before, when we finished 3rd, we missed first place by less than two seconds!

Winning by three seconds was considered a rout by canoe race standards. We celebrated and I went in to work the Keel Boats with a nice feeling and a number of congratulations by those who followed the canoe races.

Team Bad News Canoes, 1983. Just before going out and winning the first-ever "Park Championships."

The following morning would be my last morning clocking in to the Park to work on the West Side. More specifically, it would be the last time I would work Keel Boats, an attraction that I had grown to love working and one that I was fairly well known for working.

Earlier that morning, there was a first-ever held event: a handicapped race between the men, the women, and the mixed canoe teams. Canoe Race Officials thought that it would be interesting to create a race which would identify the Park Champions between the three teams. Taking the winning times in each division, our men's team was handicapped the difference between our winning time and the winning times for the mixed and women's teams.

What everyone thought was a great idea, the race was very anticlimactic. There were no fans for this race, the television news teams and newspaper reporters weren't there, and basically, none of us really wanted to go out and bust our guts one more time.

However, we did go out and raced. We were more than a little surprised that we actually won that race by a couple seconds. The event made us the first-ever Park Champions for all divisions. And perhaps, since I heard that they didn't repeat the event, we very well could be the ONLY Park Champions ever crowned!

When many employees quit Disneyland, they sometimes go out with a bang. One Jungle Cruise member, on his last day, dove from his boat and swam to the Hippo pool where he playfully attacked one of the audio-animatronic hippos in the Jungle Cruise River with a rubber knife. Others have taken swan dives into the Rivers of America from the seawall fence. Many working attractions take their pictures with some of the audio-animatronic figures in some peculiar poses!

While I had thought about how I would quit the Park, I didn't think I could improve upon winning the canoe races...twice, during my final two days.

So, I simply went home early, feeling victorious.

It was a slow day at Disneyland, anyway.

Chapter 9

Riding the Rail: The Monorail

Because of a number of reasons, I decided to rehire back into Disneyland the next summer. It was 1984.

My canoe team wanted to have a chance to repeat as champions, something that hadn't been done since the years Engulf and Devour had dominated the races in the 1970s. I also missed the Park, my friends there, all the parties, and simply put, Disneyland was a great place to work!

But, in rehiring, I was not guaranteed I would get my job in West-Side operations back. I was offered an interesting job however...one that I felt would really be a kick. I was hired to drive the Monorail.

The Disneyland Monorail was probably the most visible moving vehicle in all of Disneyland, only surpassed in iconic association with Disneyland by the Mark Twain Steamship that sails around Tom Sawyer Island.

A Disneyland Mark III Monorail loading passengers at the Disneyland Hotel. Note the bubble atop the front car, (far right), where the driver sat.
(Source: EditorASC at en.wikipedia,)

In my mind, driving the Monorail was akin to flying an airplane, only not nearly as dangerous or as complicated! However, the Monorail was the most expensive transportation system and vehicle in the Park. It was also the only one that actually traveled outside the Park. The Monorail took passengers to and from the Disneyland Hotel which was across the parking lot and across West Street to the Monorail Station at the Hotel along its 2.5 mile round-trip route.

At the time, the Monorails I was trained to operate were the Mark III versions; they had a conical nose and tail section and the driver, along with two guests, rode up in the bubble on top of the front car. 1987, the vehicles underwent a major redesign becoming Mark V models, similar to the Mark IV design of the more modern looking monorails used at Disneyworld in Florida. In 2008, they would go through another design change and color scheme, identified as Mark VII models that are in use today, as of this printing.

From 1959, the Monorail went from being the "Viewliner," a 1950's attempt at being a modern train that ran on rails around the Park alongside the Disneyland Railroad in some sections of the Park, to the raised Monorail we see today. The power-system that runs the Monorail is like a giant electric train set. The cars sit on ride-wheels upon the concrete rails that are suspended in the air upon large concrete pillars all along the Monorail path. However, unlike the train sets I grew up with, the Monorails ran on a lot more juice! Six hundred volts of direct current power the electric vehicles, using two inside contact-bars that run along the concrete beams. That electricity was delivered to the electric motors that are housed in each of the five cars that make up a single Monorail train.

Far Different than the West Side

After working so long on the other side of the Park, I could tell right from the first day of training that working in Tomorrowland on the Monorail, was going to be much different than what I had grown accustomed to in my previous five years. There was a completely different atmosphere working in Tomorrowland compared to a much more laid-back environment on the west side. The operators in Tomorrowland were far more serious, less approachable, and less outgoing than the cast members I had worked with in the years prior. There were plenty of exceptions to this generalization. It wasn't that they were not friendly, but there was a tangible lack of warmth and welcoming that I noticed right from day one.

Perhaps it was because Tomorrowland was essentially a synthetic expanse, filled with technology, concrete, metal, and plastic. There was—and still is—a sense of electric, kinetic motion all around. Compared to the natural shrubs, trees and bodies of water found on the West Side, Tomorrowland was the polar opposite. Of course, Tomorrowland had the Submarine Lagoon...but that was more like an oversized, heavily chlorinated fish tank! From the constant motion of the Peoplemover that crisscrossed above Tomorrowland to the Monorail itself, from the submarines in the sub lagoon below the Monorail track to the aerial Skyway moving overhead, there was constant motion everywhere you looked.

Additionally, the unmelodic synthesis of sound was everywhere. From the bands that played on the Tomorrowland Terrace to the engine sounds coming from the Autopia cars to the cacophony of talk from thousands of guests milling within the concrete expanse of Tomorrowland, there was a constant competition of sounds coming from everywhere! And, essentially, all of this sound had nowhere to go! Sound reverberated off the pavement and the buildings as if trapped in a giant concrete shoebox.

I had taken for granted the relative calm on the West Side where there was the openness of the area; the trees and the foliage, and the expanse of the Rivers of America surrounding Tom Sawyer Island, all of which absorbed whatever sounds were present. Music on the West Side consisted of a three-piece band playing Dixieland Jazz. And out on the canoes or Keel Boats, the back side of Tom Sawyer Island offered a resolute tranquility that was almost therapeutic. Even from way out on the River while paddling the canoe or cruising in on the Keel Boat, you could hear the only other music played in the area: polka music, which emanated from the Swiss Family Tree House. The occasional steam whistle on the Mark Twain would blow, or they would shoot off the cannon on the Columbia, offering a subtle reminder that there was indeed activity on the River.

It was within the first few days of my rehire that I came to the realization I would probably not last working in Tomorrowland or on the Monorail. In addition to this trepidation, within a month of my return to Disneyland, my father passed away in late June, a sudden death that marked—and marred—the summer of 1984 for me.

It was as if I suddenly knew I had made a mistake in coming back to Disneyland to work. Even my canoe team, BNC, we shortened the name from Bad News Canoes to just the acronym, for some unknown reason, did very poorly. We finished fourth out of the four teams that raced in the finals that year, making it my worst finish ever in the Canoe Races in my five years competing.

At the time, I had just finished my second year of teaching at Garden Grove High School. I had established a band that was becoming popular throughout Orange County and beyond. I was a bass player for a band I organized called Max which played night clubs in Long Beach and Orange County, as well as large dorm parties at UCLA and a few other schools. While I don't think at the time I would have admitted it, I found I was not looking forward to coming to work at Disneyland like I had in my previous years.

Unlike the positive expectations upon being told I would be working on the Monorail when I was rehired, driving the Monorail turned out to be very mundane. I had anticipated being at the helm of the sleek, futuristic vehicles would be very rewarding, or at least, very cool. Instead, it actually felt like work.

One of the many reasons I was unhappy was that working on the Monorail, there was almost no interaction directly with guests as I had enjoyed on the Canoes, Keel Boats, or even on Pirates of the Caribbean. While driving the Monorail, we had no spiel to give except a short,

"Ladies and gentlemen, if you plan to leave Disneyland today and wish to return, please remember to have your hand stamped at the hotel exit or at the Main Gate.

Disneyland is open until midnight tonight. Thank you and have a wonderful day here at Disneyland."

Occasionally, just for kicks, I would substitute "Knott's Berry Farm" for "Disneyland" at the end of the spiel, and then add, "Oh, I mean Disneyland." It was the only time I got to hear laughter while working on the Monorail. And even that, it was muffled as I could only hear people in the first car behind me or the few people in the front driver's cab with me. On the Monorail, there were no jokes to tell, and really, no fellow cast members to interact with. On Monorail, you either worked the Platform at the Hotel or the Tomorrowland Station, or you were driving a Monorail, none of which offered the kind of interaction I was missing.

Technically, the Monorail was easy to drive. There was a T-Bar, similar to a stick shift in a car, which controlled the speed of the trains. There were four forward speeds, which you moved the T-Bar forward for. To go backwards, you pulled the T-Bar backwards where there were two speeds in reverse. And to stop, you pulled back hard on the T-Bar which activated the air breaks in each car. Sometimes, if you were coming into one of the monorail platforms too fast, you had to pull the T-Bar with both hands as the air brakes responded to how hard you pulled back on the T-Bar!

There was a Dead-man Disengage button on the top of the T-Bar that had to be held down throughout the trip. If you lifted your hand off the button, the Monorail's brakes would be slowly engaged and the Monorail would come to a stop. The idea was that if the driver suddenly collapsed or somehow died while the Monorail was in motion, the driver's hand would fall off the T-bar and off the button causing the Monorail to stop. This was to prevent the Monorail from running into a parked Monorail if something like this did indeed happen to the driver.

Also, the driver was responsible to press a small button on the side control panel that turned on each recorded spiel for the

Monorail based on specific locations along the track. It would point out things or give background on the ride itself. Right below this button was an intercom to address the guests on the Monorail. And a third button in this set was a walkie-talkie for calling the main Monorail control office and security. Occasionally, a driver would inadvertently press the walkie-talkie button to address the guests, sending their spiel instead to the office and to the security channels.

About the only excitement I had was my final day working the Monorail. It was the one and only time that I was asked to move a Monorail off the main track and into the Monorail garage. Since it was my last day—and it was a slow day—I was asked to take Monorail Red off the main line before I left to clock out—for good. I said, "Sure," as if I had done it a dozen times. Actually, I was desperately trying to remember the procedure for doing it since I had been shown how to do it only once, when I was being trained two months earlier.

Surprisingly, I was able to remember to drive Big Red to the switch track. I remembered to radio the control office to switch the track. After getting the green light on the switch track signal, I slowly accelerated the Monorail into the garage where a mechanic inside on the cat walk directed me to where to stop the Monorail so the train was all the way inside.

Stepping out of the Monorail for the last time as a cast member, I felt a little twinge of nostalgia. Not because I was leaving the Monorail for good, but because I knew I was leaving *Disneyland* for good. I knew in my heart I was not coming back.

I have very few memories of working on the Monorail. I know I did feel a sense of pride when I was up in the bubble driving the different colored Monorails; people looking up, waving, and seeing the big, unique vehicle sail by on its futuristic concrete track.

169

I do remember leaving that final day working at Disneyland; changing out of my blue Monorail costume for the last time, turning it in to wardrobe, walking down the sloped walkway under the Disneyland Railroad tracks, heading into Harbor House, pushing my time card into the time clock to punch out for the very last time. I remember telling the guard at the employee entrance: "have a nice day;" him saluting me as if he somehow knew it was indeed my last time passing through that point of transition from the world of fantasy and make-believe back into the world of reality.

Life for me moved on in a new direction after that day.

Yet, Disneyland had a few more tricks up its sleeve for me.

Oh, ironically, it wouldn't be the last time I would drive a monorail. Only the next time I did it, it was on the east coast!

The Year, Going From Bad to Worse

I had a pretty bad year and a half, starting with my grandmother passing away in late 1983. Then my father passed away of a sudden heart attack. Perhaps that was a more distinctive reason I didn't have a great experience working at Disneyland that particular summer. My father and I were planning to coach together at La Quinta High School that coming year...instead I took over his tennis program and even started teaching high school in the very same classroom that he had taught in. Then later in December, five months after I had left Disneyland, a woman ran a red light and broad-sided my 280ZX knocking me unconscious. I had four broken ribs and internal bleeding. I was in the hospital for a week.

After the accident, I woke up in the very same hospital emergency room that my father had died in a two months before. When my mother came in to see me for the first time, I remember thinking that she looked like a wreck, which, in hindsight, was probably exactly how she felt about having to see her semi-conscious son laying in the same room that she had last seen her husband in.

That same week, my grandfather died from what I think was a broken heart after losing his wife and son-in-law, and maybe hearing about me in the hospital, all within a period of 12 months.

I returned to the living after the Christmas holiday, not the most joyous Christmas that particular year, I remember. But, the year was finally over. I looked forward to what I hoped would be a much more enjoyable 1985.

Chapter 10

Post Cast Member Years

My first five years working at Disneyland were full of adventure, friendship, and memories. Even my final year of driving the Disneyland Monorail had its moments. Many of my closest friendships developed from friends I worked with during those years. I know for all who had enjoyed working at Disneyland, a bond had been formed that linked the Park to the many friendships and memories that directly resulted from our time spent as cast members within that Shadow of the Matterhorn.

In addition to time spent working attractions, many of us were also trained to work guest control during parades and shows. The River Stage was a challenge back when it was first developed. We brought out thousands of folding chairs and set up viewing areas along the river wall, unfolding each chair and sending it sliding along the walkway to another cast member who would catch it and align it with the other chairs in a row. Today, people simply sit on the ground during the newer show, *Fantasmic!*

Occasionally, we had interesting events occur during such shows. I remember a young lady coming up to me and asking me if I had a friend...and if I had a break coming up. She and a friend wanted to get to know us better in the span of fifteen minutes!

Oftentimes, you would come to work with a premonition, a feeling that it was going to be an even more bizarre day at Disneyland than the norm. And usually, we would be correct in having those ominous feelings. The river would close because the Mark Twain broke down or we would meet someone very intriguing, or, a more gruesome premonition, someone would die.

In addition to the death that I was directly involved in discovering, I also was working the night in 1980 when an eighteen-year-old man was killed on the PeopleMover. During my second year working, a woman died after riding Space Mountain.

We paid attention to our ominous feelings.

Working Canoes and Keel Boats was like having a barometer to gauge the type of guests the Park would have that day. Some days the Park was filled with guests who were dull and unmoved by anything you said. Other days, guests were ready to explode with laughter. The weather had a lot to do with that condition. On warm sunny days, people tended to be ready for fun. On cloudy, overcast, or rainy days they were just the opposite. However, I always enjoyed working over the Christmas holidays regardless of the weather. Disneyland is known for dressing up the Park for most holidays, Christmas being the most elaborate. We wore coats and mufflers, and sometimes even gloves, which seems weird as the weather in Southern California is not known for unseasonably cold weather. But, like our occasional hot summer days, winter could blast us with wind chill and moisture too.

Christmas at the Park was like having a second Family Christmas for most cast members. It was rare that I didn't work at Disneyland on Christmas Day. I remember my family always planning our family Christmas around our scheduled shifts at the Park.

During the holidays, friends would exchange gifts. Others brought a multitude of goodies, from cookies to brownies to fudge and there were many days many of us were operating on sugar highs and chocolate overdoses. Working the Canoes back then was great since we could work off whatever we ate.

Since those years, now over twenty-five years later, there have been numerous cast member reunions. These gatherings provided many former Disneyland cast members the opportunity to revisit those delightful years working at the Park. Many of us have reconnected with those we spent countless hours making magic at the Magic Kingdom. Thanks to the Internet, there are dozens of web pages dedicated to former cast members as well as social networks that allow us to stay in touch, even as some of us have moved great distances from Disneyland.

The year following my departure from Disneyland, I established our band MAX, which became a popular cover band for several night clubs in Southern California. Fate came into play for two of us in the band that year.

Ironically, Disneyland still had a hand, indirectly, in my life. My keyboard player, Grant, the same Grant that was my partner on the canoes the day I got the $5 tip from the family who we let splash five years earlier, still worked at Disneyland. His canoe team, *Rock and Row* became the dominant team for a number of years. Grant devised new ways to do switches with his teams that have since become standard in the races. He has moved up in the organization, making Disneyland his career.

The twist of fate that I mentioned, involved several things that had to occur.

Our band was asked to play a Friday, Saturday and Sunday night gig at a place right down the street from Disneyland. It was called, "Mississippi Moonshine Meat and Music Company." The night club, being so close to the Park, was a draw for our friends who still worked there.

The first fateful event was that a guy who owned a night club near Knott's Berry Farm in Buena Park, about eight miles from Disneyland, was supposed to go hear a different band playing at some other night club in Anaheim. He ended up getting lost and saw the Mississippi night club with the sign, "LIVE MUSIC." Considering he had come to hear a band play that he was considering for his night club, he figured he might get lucky and find a band in this other club.

That night, he liked what he heard and gave his card to Kirk, our drummer, who proceeded to forget all about the man and his business card for several days!

Five days later, we had our regular band rehearsal at our practice studio and Kirk pulled out the business card he had been given and handed it to Joe, our lead guitar player.

"Oh, I forgot this guy came up to me at Mississippi Meat and Music last Saturday and gave me his card. He said something about wanting us to play at his nightclub."

Joe, who was the only real full-time musician in the band almost freaked out. Immediately, Joe contacted the man and found out he owned a club called "Cartoons and Capers", a '50's – '60's style night club, and the man wanted us to play for two weeks with the possibility of doing many more weeks if we sustained the crowd. And he wanted us to start this coming Tuesday!

The only stipulation was we needed to learn a bunch of 50's and 60's type songs to go along with our repertoire of current top-40 hits. So, we added about fifteen older songs to go with our 70's and 80's hits. We had a song list of 40 songs a night, with ten more upbeat songs thrown in on Friday and Saturday nights when the crowds were expected to be bigger and more lively.

About four months later we were not only still playing at Cartoons as their house band, four weeks on, two weeks off, but the club was packed most nights. We were a band that included humor mixed in with quality cover songs. In reality, we were a band that didn't try hard to be a rock band. We just had fun playing quality music!

At Cartoons and Capers, about two weeks before Christmas, my drummer Kirk and I met the women would end up becoming our future wives.

The funniest story was when Kirk met Kathy. They met at the night club during a band-break when the House DJ was spinning some records to keep the place hopping between sets of live music. After about fifteen minutes, Kirk told Kathy he had to go. She told him it was nice meeting him. Kirk melded into the crowd on his way up to the stage to start the next set of music. Because the drums were up on a drum riser, on top of the stage, most people could hardly see Kirk from behind his cymbals and toms making up the front of his drum kit.

Forty-five minutes later, when we took our next break, Kathy was still there. Kirk went up to her and they started talking again. She was surprised to see Kirk had returned. After another fifteen minutes, Kirk, of course, told her he had to go again.

"Why do you have to keep leaving?" Kathy asked a little confused by his need to depart; she had no idea he was the drummer in the band.

Kirk, pointing to the stage said, "Um, I have to go drum...I'm the drummer..."

A little embarrassed, Kathy nodded. "OOhh. Now I get it!"

Kathy stayed and danced, this time peeking at Kirk from between the drums and cymbals during each song.

A couple days later, I was sitting with TJ, our lead singer in one of the booths at Cartoons and Capers, about twenty minutes before our first set. As we talked, I glanced up and saw a couple of attractive women walk into the club. Jokingly, I pointed toward the women when they pulled up seats at the counter surrounding the dance floor. I said, "Hey, TJ, I think I'm going to marry that one girl right there." I pointed to a slender brunette wearing black pants and a sweater top. At the night club, we got all kinds of men and women. Yet this woman wearing a very conservative outfit, stood out to me at that moment. Probably because the place was still quiet, I'd been able to spot the two coming in without distraction.

I didn't give the woman much more thought as we played our first set of music. It was a Friday night and the crowd was lively, typical for kicking off the weekend. Grant had a few friends from Disneyland at the night club that evening. During our first break, I was chatting with a couple of his friends. However, I caught sight of the woman who I had spotted earlier.

Excusing myself from Grant's friends, I walked to the bar to order a beverage, walking by the woman I'd seen earlier. She was holding a shot glass in her hand, sort of studying the liquid inside, wondering perhaps if it was lethal.

I smiled at her and said, "It isn't too bad," referring to the Kamikaze she held. The band was often bought Kamikaze shots by appreciative members in the crowd or by friends of ours, so I knew how the drinks tasted.

Smiling back at me, she said, "I'll drink half if you drink half."

It was an invitation that I couldn't refuse...even if the man who I guess bought the drink for her was standing a few feet away.

In just over nine months, this woman at the club, Kerri, became my wife, making my proclamation to TJ—even if I had been joking at the time—a reality!

Kirk ended up marrying Kathy too, about a year after I married Kerri.

Honeymoon

Of course, Disney would come back into my life...only this time, it was Disneyworld, and this time, it was a much more joyous occasion: My honeymoon!

August 8th, 1987 I married Kerri in Tustin, California. Our honeymoon was a cruise to the Bahamas and four days at Walt Disney's Magic Kingdom in Florida, Walt Disney World.

A Mark VI Monorail at Disneyworld.

We had a glorious time on both the cruise and the Disneyworld trip. Ironically, and it wasn't even planned, we got to sit up in the front of one of the Monorails. It transported guests to and from the Parks, the parking and transportation center, and to various Disney hotels along one of the Monorail lines. Unlike the Mark III Monorails I had driven at Disneyland, the newer Mark V Monorails used throughout Disneyworld, featured a captain's chair on the floor of the front car and a futuristic computer console from which the Monorail Captain could operate not only his Monorail, but it displayed the entire Monorail system on a full-color monitor, allowing the driver to know exactly where each Monorail was located, speeds of each, etc. In chatting with the captain of the Monorail my wife and I were on, I mentioned that I used to drive the Mark III Monorails at Disneyland. Obviously a less strict working environment than what cast members are used to today, the captain asked if I would like to drive that Monorail. It did feature the same T-Bar acceleration stick and power options that our Monorails at Disneyland had.) I was thrilled to be allowed to drive if for just a few minutes along one of the longer stretches of track. The Monorails at Disneyworld were much faster, allowed to go nearly 50 miles per hour, compared to the 28 to 32 mph that the Disneyland Monorails were governed to not exceed.

The Mark VI Control Console. Note the "T" Bar on the far right and the "E-Stop" Button near the center of the lower panel.

I had kept my Disneyland ID card and I was actually surprised that the cast member at River Country, a waterpark at Disneyworld, allowed us to get in for free because I had it with me.

I enjoyed the chance to show Kerri both the Magic Kingdom and the newer EPCOT Park that was part of Disneyworld.

Back during the summer of 1982, myself and about four hundred other Disneyland cast members were given the chance to go to Disneyworld as part of a special cast member program. For only four-hundred dollars, we received airfare, hotel and admissions to Disneyworld for a week. Myself and about fifteen of my closest cast member friends went on the trip and had a great time. We were also given tours of the complex underground portions of Disneyworld and all the latest technology that went into building those Parks.

Now, five years later, I got to go to Disneyworld as a guest, but this time as a married guest. My wife and I had the time of our lives!

It would be 2003 that we would return to Disneyworld, 16 years later, this time taking our four year-old daughter, Kyla and my mom and her new husband, Bill with us. Disneyland had just set sail with their new cruise line, Disney Cruise Line, and two new ships, the **Disney Wonder** and the **Disney Magic.**

On our honeymoon, the cruise ship we took was the Oceanic, also known at that time as the "Big Red Boat" since its hull was painted completely red. It was a nice ship for the day but Disney now upped the ante with not only spectacular ships, but cutting edge programs for kids, adults, and amenities aboard both ships that only Disney could pull off.

You have to understand that a Disneyworld Vacation is seldom a 'vacation'...in the relaxing sense of the word. With only four days on land, (as opposed to a non-cruise vacation that might include seven or more days), you try to get in all you can. On our honeymoon, the cruise was first, the Disneyworld portion was the last four days. We returned home happy, yet exhausted. Instead, today Disney fashions Land/Sea packages so that the cruise is usually last, allowing the guests to go to the Parks for three or four days, (or longer if people want to add days to their trip), and then cruise for three or four days and now they offer seven day cruises. In my opinion, the cruise is the perfect climax to the entire vacation because you are able to relax, eat fabulous meals in different restaurants on board, be pampered, and do as much—or as little—as you want!

We have since taken our third Disney Cruise vacation with our daughter who was now nine years old, and her younger brother, Keaton, who had just turned four.

We have been on other cruise ships and they all have kids programs that are usually pretty good. But, compared to the Disney Cruise ships, they can't come close. On board the Disney ships, your kids can be involved in kids programs from 9am until

2am the next morning! And, as we—and our kids discovered—the programs are far better designed, keeping the kids excited and literally wanting to be in the kids programs far more than on other ships.

Grad Nite

During the next few years, I personally don't remember going to Disneyland. It wasn't until I took over teaching and coaching at LaQuinta High School that I ended up back at Disneyland.

Grad Nite as a cast member was always interesting. However, now, as a teacher—and a chaperone for our graduating seniors at LaQuinta High School—I got to revisit Disneyland, this time, as a guest, sort of! Each school had to provide a certain number of chaperones based on the number of students from that school who were attending that particular Grad Nite. I welcomed the chance to return to the Park as a chaperone for the students at La Quinta High School. My wife and I and a number of fellow teachers attended the all-night party. The nice thing was, the teachers that got to go didn't have to pay. Because each school had to have at least one chaperone in the chaperone headquarters at all times, the teachers attending took shifts of about ninety minutes, drinking coffee and hanging out with other teachers from other schools at the chaperone headquarters. With about four teachers and their spouses, that gave each of us about four hours to enjoy the Park before having to spend our 90 minutes on staff at the headquarters pavilion.

Unlike the night when I was involved with finding the dead boy drowned in the River, thankfully, the Grad Nites we attended were relatively uneventful.

I did get to sneak my wife into some of the off-limit, backstage areas of the Park where I used to work, taking her to see some of the underground passages below Pirates and Haunted

Mansion. I even stole a kiss from her upon the steps of that led down below the Haunted Mansion attraction!

In a few years, I would move to Arizona and it would be another ten years almost before I would return to the Magic Kingdom.

Chapter 11

Fifty Years...and Counting!

On July 17th, 2005, Disneyland turned fifty years old.

Three years later, on July 21st, 2008, I turned fifty years old.

Twenty-four years passed since I had worked at Disneyland. As most people who reach their fifties can attest, time seemed to be ticking away faster and faster. My kids were growing like weeds, my knees were starting to hurt more and every time I played tennis; my back was always an issue, and wrinkles were appearing on my face. They say "50 is the new 40". Tell that to my back and my joints!

But then, all my friends who were my age were going through the same things.

One thing about going to Disneyland when you are older is the sense of remembering the feelings you had when you visited the Park as a youngster or as a young adult. Subconsciously or consciously, we replay snippets of memories as we stroll through Disneyland or go on various attractions.

There really is a kid in all of us. Disneyland personifies not just the sense of adventure that Walt Disney wanted his guests to experience at his little Park, but there is a sense of nostalgia many of us experience when revisiting the Park. Perhaps it is this opportunity to reminisce that brings out that kid in us every time we visit a Disney Park.

There are two nostalgias I consider Disneyland provides. One, the simple nostalgia that Walt Disney wanted to preserve when he designed Main Street USA, a desire to revisit his own boyhood town, the sense of community, patriotism, and family.

The second nostalgia is that which Disneyland itself creates for every single individual who may have visited the Park at a young age. Obviously, visits later in life will summon memories of those early visits, taking us consciously—or unconsciously, back in time. Like any joyous or happy event, opportunities that trigger memories of that event usually are also memorable and pleasing.

Now with two young children, I felt that sense of nostalgia when I first took my then six year-old daughter to Disneyland, and all the times after with her and then her little brother. I remember walking through one of the two tunnels at the entrance of the Park, emerging onto Main Street and the vista it provided. I remember my anticipation of the day, looking across the plaza square at the kinetic motion of people and Main Street vehicles. I admired the well-planned architecture drawing my attention just as it did that first time I went to Disneyland. Yes, I was living vicariously through my daughter's first visit, and later my son's. But that is what Disneyland is all about to me. Maybe that is what Walt Disney really had in mind when he said he "wanted to build something for the entire family."

Perhaps that's why so many families make annual treks to Disneyland. Some even more often! The opportunity to revisit those nostalgic feelings, of immersing yourself in a world of make-believe, seeing things we are familiar with; or, perhaps, we love to just see what's new!

I've been on Space Mountain at least a hundred times in my life. I still love the attraction. I know every turn and drop of the ride and look forward to each as our vehicle accelerates faster and faster. When they added new special effects and a thrilling soundtrack to the experience, suddenly the familiar also became new for me. I love talking about each attraction with my children; we share our favorite parts, talk about going on it again, etc.

I can board the Mark Twain and feel my blood pressure drop, my breathing slow, and my mind relax. There is something about hearing that steam whistle blow that sends me back to the late 1970s when I worked on the River and would hear that whistle blow many times each day.

I still hear that whistle blow even now, as I live four-hundred miles away. Not the actual whistle of course, but I catch myself hearing something in the distance, something that is in the same key as the Mark Twain's whistle, and for a brief instant, I'm back at Disneyland.

Left: *Hidden Mickey: Sometimes Dead Men DO Tell Tales* was the first book of the HIDDEN MICKEY series. The book is the story of two men who stumble upon Walt Disney's lost diary, a diary that hints of hidden treasure that Walt Disney may have left behind to be found.

Right: *Hidden Mickey 2: It All Started…* follows a missed clue from the first book which leads to an amazing discovery. However, another person also seeks the mysterious Disney cache!

When I came up with the idea for the book *HIDDEN MICKEY*, I saw the potential for a clue-driven treasure hunt surrounding Walt Disney. After seeing the movie *National Treasure* and reading Dan Brown's book *The DaVinci Code*, I suddenly sat bolt upright in bed one night and thought to myself, "Who in the world would have had the foresight and imagination to perhaps leave a trail of clues that would lead to something very valuable?" WALT DISNEY came to my mind that instant.

This was in 2008. While I had been to Disneyland and Disneyworld several times over the 21 years since my wife and I first got married, I honestly didn't think much about the Park or about Walt Disney a lot during those two decades. I did read many books about Walt Disney over the years. In fact, my collection of nearly 25 books on Disney kept me in the loop, even as I wasn't as consciously thinking about the man or his Parks over those years. I still marvel at the accomplishments Walt experienced, but, perhaps more poignant to me was the mindset that Walt seemed to maintain, even in the midst of multiple failures early in his career.

The most enduring tale of Walt was his response to those who told him he would fail. His response was revealing:

"I never get mad at people when they don't embrace my ideas or say they won't work. I just smile at them knowing that simply, they don't see it the way I do."

While I've paraphrased Walt here from several books that have quoted Walt Disney, the concept is clear: Walt was confident in his own understanding of human nature and what, at the time, people wanted. He never got mad at those who said he would fail or that his ideas wouldn't work. On the contrary, Walt Disney believed that all the naysayers would agree if only they saw things the way HE DID! Of course, how many people had the vision and belief in themselves to the degree Walt Disney did?

Because I first shared my idea of the book concept of *HIDDEN MICKEY* with my friend, Nancy Temple Rodrigue, she immediately took the idea and began drafting a story from my thoughts, adding ideas and characters of her own along the way. Like me, Nancy was well-read on all things Disney. Nancy was also a true Disney aficionado, owning hundreds of collectable and unique Disney items, all displayed in her writing office. Thus, the first two *HIDDEN MICKEY* novels were collaboration, the blending of two imaginations into two very popular books!

Also motivating me was that I had always wanted to do a book like David Koenig's fanciful book, *Mouse Tales*, a book where he captured intriguing and funny stories from hundreds of cast-member interviews and then depicted them within excellent prose and storytelling.

HIDDEN MICKEY 5: Chasing New Frontiers was the last of our HIDDEN MICKEY novels; it was a solo effort in the series and a book that I thoroughly enjoyed writing since the main character, Blain Walters, was basically an extension of my life working at Disneyland. Nearly everything that happens to Blain happened to me while working at Disneyland!

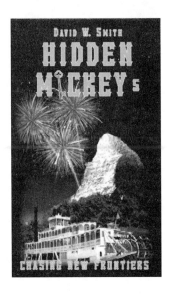

The Cover of Hidden Mickey 5: Chasing New Frontiers.

The story is of charismatic Blain Walters meeting a beautiful Swiss visitor, Missy Johansen. The young couple stumbles upon a 44-year old lost wallet and embark on an unforgettable treasure hunt at Disneyland!
www.synergy-books.com
www.amazon.com

What Lies Ahead?

There is no preconceived notion of what Disneyland and Walt Disney have in store for me in the future. Perhaps, this is the last of what I might write about the man and my experiences with his Disneyland.

Maybe this book will encourage others who have worked for Walt Disney or worked at Disneyland, to share their intimate and individual stories about their own experiences.

My hope is that I've made you chuckle, reminisce, and understand more about the human side of working at Disneyland. If I've accomplished those things, then I feel I've succeeded!

Most of all, this book is a personal memoire of one who truly lived in the Shadow of the Matterhorn.

The End.

About The Author

David W. Smith

David W. Smith is the author of Hidden Mickey 5 as well as author of Hidden Mickey 1 & 2 with co-author, Nancy Temple Rodrigue.

As *In the Shadow of the Matterhorn* reveals, David spent six years working at Disneyland in Anaheim. In addition, Dave was a school teacher, teaching Advanced Biology and Human Biology as well as a variety of other science classes while living in Southern California. Later, he taught school and coached tennis, golf and badminton in Arizona while his wife finished her medical school and residency training.

David is the author of two of the top-selling tennis instructional books, *Tennis Mastery* (2004) & *Coaching Mastery* (2008). David W. Smith is also the Senior Editor for one of the top-rated tennis web sites in the world. (TennisOne.com) Considered as one of the premier tennis teachers in the U.S., David has been selected by Wilson Racquet Sports, Prince Sports and Dunlop Racquet Sports to be one of their Premier, Elite and Master Tennis Professionals (respectfully) representing each company at various times over the past fifteen years. David is one of about 20 tennis pros to have reached this level of recognition in the world.

David has published over 300 articles in a wide range of domestic and European publications. He has produced the DVDs, "Building a World-Class Volley" and "The Ultimate Serve Tune-Up." In addition, David has given lectures and workshops all around the U.S. on tennis as well as on writing.

In addition to writing, Dave is a professional musician playing bass and guitar. Most recently Dave plays contemporary Christian music with his band, "The Vinyard." He also has played bass guitar with the teen sensation, Carlie Wall on her first concert tour in 2010. In the early 1980's David played guitar and bass for a number of bands, including his own band MAX, a band that played many venues around Disneyland and throughout Southern California.

David is also a professional magician, having performed for large and small audiences. Specializing in close up magic, David also has formed many programs for teaching magic to youngsters and adults alike.

David has been married for 24 years to Dr. Kerri Smith, a pediatrician. David, Kerri and their two children, Kyla Marie who is thirteen and Keaton Bruce who is nine, along with three dogs, two guinea pigs and one cat, all reside in the beautiful red-rock scenery of St. George, Utah.

Books and DVDs by David W. Smith
All products available through Synergy-Books.com

Top left to right: Hidden Mickey 5, Hidden Mickey 1, Hidden Mickey 2, Tennis Mastery; Bottom row: Coaching Mastery, Building A World-Class Volley (DVD), TennisOne Tune-up: The Serve (DVD)

Hidden Mickey 5: Chasing New Frontiers

In the last **Hidden Mickey** novel, David W. Smith takes readers on a quest for long-lost stolen cash and Walt Disney's legendary Red Diamond Pendant. **Hidden Mickey 5** introduces Blain Walters, a charismatic Disneyland Cast Member and Missy Johansen, a beautiful, adventuresome Swiss visitor to the Magic Kingdom where they find that fate has brought them together. When Blain shows Missy a secret location inside the Park, the two stumble upon a very old wallet...a wallet that literally contains a key to a nearly half-century old mystery. While following clues to the missing money and mysterious pendant the young couple find a real connection to each other.

Hidden Mickey: Sometimes Dead Men DO Tell Tales

The book that started the series, this first *Hidden Mickey* follows best friends, Adam and Lance, as they stumble upon Walt Disney's lost diary...a diary that hints of a treasure and a cryptic clue. The journal sends the two friends on a wild, cross-country quest seeking additional clues that Walt Disney hid. In addition, the two friends must enlist the help of Adam's former girlfriend, Beth, a woman who Adam had accidently gotten fired from her beloved job at Disneyland. Not having spoken to each other in five years, Adam and Beth must put their past behind them and work together to solve Walt's mystery. With co-author Nancy Temple Rodrigue.

Hidden Mickey 2: It All Started...

The amazing sequel to the first book, *Hidden Mickey 2* follows a missed clue that would have taken Lance and Adam to uncharted territories! This time, Lance finds himself at the dangerous end of a 44 Magnum! He must befriend a beautiful blonde named Kimberly, the daughter of the only man to have been privy to Walt Disney's secrets. However, Kimberly and Lance find a dangerous advisory who is bent on not only finding Walt's treasure, but wants to destroy Walt Disney's legacy and empire in the process. With co-author Nancy Temple Rodrigue.

Tennis Mastery & Coaching Mastery

Two of the top-selling and highly-acclaimed instructional books for tennis players and those who teach tennis! *Tennis Mastery* introduced the Advanced Foundation training principles that David Smith used to train thousands of top-level players. *Coaching Mastery* is the Ultimate Blueprint for tennis coaches, tennis parents, and tennis teaching professionals. *Coaching Mastery* documents the methods that David and his father Bruce Smith used to in creating one of the most successful tennis teams in the U.S.

DVDs: Building a World-Class Volley & TennisOne Tune-Up The Serve

Produced by TennisOne.com and starring David W. Smith, these two DVDs focus on the finest methods and most current modern systems to develop the Volley and the Serve.

Building a World-Class Volley is over 2 hours and covers every type of volley as well as providing tips and drills that will improve every part of your volley fast!

TennisOne Tune-up: the Serve teaches all the different types of serves, how to develop spin, speed, and consistency, and ultimately, make any serve a WEAPON!